The Economics of Higher Education

Affordability & Access;
Costing, Pricing & Accountability

David Palfreyman

David Palfreyman is the Bursar of and a Fellow of New College, Oxford, and the Director of the Oxford Centre for Higher Education Policy Studies (OxCHEPS) a 'think-tank' independent of both New College and the University of Oxford. He is the author, with Ted Tapper, of *Oxford and the Decline of the Collegiate Tradition* and editor, with David Warner, of *Higher Education Management* and of *Higher Education Law*, as well as being general co-editor of the Open University Press/McGraw-Hill fifteen volume *Managing Universities and Colleges* series.

The author is grateful to the following: Ian Laing for his generous financial support in the creation of OxCHEPS; Sir David Davies as the driving-force behind, and a major funder of, the 'Costing, Funding and Sustaining Oxford' research project; Nicholas Ulanov and Alexander Sherman as the consultants from The Ulanov Partnership working on that project; and the Institute of Higher Education, University of Georgia, Athens, USA, for financing a visit to the IHE in the Spring of 2003 which enabled much of the material for this book to be gathered. As always, the author remains thankful for his good fortune in working amongst such supportive colleagues at New College, notably Alan Ryan as Warden and Kate Hunter as Bursar's Secretary; and, in the context of writing a book on the financing of universities in the twenty-first century, also offers appreciation to William of Wykeham, the Founder of New College in 1379, whose substantial permanent endowment still some 625 years later provides crucial financial and academic independence for its Warden and Fellows in fulfilling the Founder's eleemosynary intentions within the fertile, and indeed at times febrile, federal structure of the collegiate university that is modern Oxford.

Oxford Centre for Higher Education Policy Studies

The Economics of Higher Education

Affordability & Access;
Costing, Pricing & Accountability

David Palfreyman, MA MBA LLB
Bursar & Fellow, New College, Oxford
Director, OxCHEPS

OxCHEPS, Oxford, 2004

Oxford Centre for Higher Education Policy Studies (OxCHEPS),
New College, Oxford, OX1 3BN, United Kingdom.
http://oxcheps.new.ox.ac.uk/

Published by OxCHEPS.

ISBN 0 9547433 0 X Hardback
ISBN 0 9547433 1 8 Paperback

Printed by Lightening Source, Milton Keynes, United Kingdom.
Typeset by Windrush Publishing Services, Gloucestershire.
Cover design by Roger Locke, Witney, Oxon.

CONTENTS

PREFACE

After the Commons debate of 27 January 2004 on the second reading of the Higher Education Bill, where the Government scraped by with a humiliating margin of just five votes, the furore over the future and funding of UK universities has faded into the relative calmness of the Lords (the Government margin at the third reading on 31 March being a respectable 61). As the dust settles on the 2003 White Paper on Higher Education and on the 2004 Higher Education Bill, and assuming the Bill will by July indeed have become an Act, we are left with a rather small and very tentative step having been taken, albeit a step in exactly the right direction and towards the deregulation and marketisation of HE, towards its denationalisation and (re)privatisation, towards the beginning of its Americanisation and away from the bleak prospect of its increased Europeanisation.

This book explores the economics of financing universities in the UK and in the USA, and considers how national HE systems in delivering the teaching of undergraduates as their largest cost determine the difficult balancing of the degree of public funding as a burden upon the taxpayer as against the level of a private contribution from the student/family through tuition fees.

The HE debate of 2003/04 has certainly raised the temperature; there has been much heat but depressingly little light. The following extracts from *Hansard* (Commons, 27/2/04, columns 167-281) give the flavour of the politics surrounding HE, and amply justify the comment from Simon Jenkins (*Times*, 28/1/04): 'The student fees argument has become a bundle of nonsense wrapped in humbug enveloped in class prejudice.' Or, as a *Financial Times* leader (26/3/04) commented: 'The fees debate is much ado about far too little...a heated debate over illusory principles...The current parliamentary fracas is both foolish and irrelevant...'

Extracting from *Hansard* in column order...

> ...the key issue is the fact that the massive, vicious class differential in our higher education system has remained consistent. We must attack that...ensure that the appalling obscenity of the deep class difference that affects people who go to our

1

universities is addressed and attacked. That is what the Office for Fair Access is about. (The Secretary of State for Education and Skills, Charles Clarke, col.171.)

The Bill gives Ministers the power to decide who goes to which university...It brings all universities under tighter political control than ever before. It will inflict damage on our universities, including those that aspire to be world class.' (Tim Yeo, col. 187/188.)

I passionately believe the 'marketisation' of higher education is wrong – for me it is a matter of not only economics and funding but of social justice and social cohesion. (Nicholas Brown, col. 193.)

Mention of debt aversion really irritates me. It is old fashioned, patronising and condescending: the assumption seems to be, "Working class people don't really know how to handle money. That's why they've got so little." They know how to handle money all right. And they know a bargain when they see one. Higher education is a bargain. (Jim Dowd, col. 204/205.)

The Government are wrong if they do not believe that there will be a greater call on the taxpayer to invest in a higher education system that really competes with the best in the world. (Barry Sheerman, chair of the Education Select Committee, col. 209.)

This extraordinary control-freakery in pursuit of a social, rather than an academic, agenda has never been seen in this country before. (Gillian Shepard, col. 213, referring to the Bill's proposed Office for Fair Access.)

Funding universities is not rocket science. Looking around the world, it is obvious that there are only two ways to go... One option is that the taxpayer pays the lot and fails to pay enough. That is the European system, which has resulted in the decline of what were once the finest universities in the world, in Berlin, Paris and Heidelberg. Where are they now? This is the path that we, too, have been treading over the past three decades, with the same dismal consequences staring us all in the face. The other option is mixed funding, whereby the taxpayer funding is topped up by student fees. That is the basis of the immensely successful American university system. It has been introduced successfully in Australia and is being debated and developed in many other countries. (Robert Jackson, col. 230/231.)

I believe that the only logic in the Bill is that of the Russell group – a move to a market in higher education – but what has happened is that, because Labour Members have been brave and the rebellion has been strong, concessions have been made. These concessions are welcome and good, but they are an attempt to try to squeak through a deeply flawed Bill, whose logic will drive us forward, as soon as it can be attained, to variable top-up fees and a market in higher education that will have lots of destructive effects. (Clare Short, col. 249.)

Let me tell the right hon. Lady that if the Bill fell, the universities would be in a vacuum. Some of them would go independent and others would concentrate on attracting overseas students where there are variable fees. That would diminish the number of places at our best universities for domestic students. (Ian Taylor, col. 253.)

So, has the Great Debate now ended, with universities firmly off the political agenda until the Government's promised review of fee levels in 2009 and hence the 2003/04 cap on the £3000 variable tuition fee not to be increased by more than RPI until 2012, if even by then and if at all? If so, we can expect the world-class status of Oxford, Cambridge, Imperial, the LSE and UCL to wither away into under-resourced mediocrity. The message of this book is that the debate on HE must not now be prematurely silenced, that the row is not to be covered over by a messy political fudge arising from a botched bill. Instead, we need immediately to begin the process of engaging in a new and realistic debate, of reaching this time around and long before 2009 a rational, evidence-based decision on the proper funding of UK universities, and especially if we care about the country remaining a global player in higher education, research, science and technology.

And this time around the 'top' universities, in honouring and protecting their autonomy and in taking a firmer grip of their destiny, must present much more of a united front, providing collectively the vision, leadership and strategic direction for ensuring their own continued international success, while combining academic rigour in teaching with equality of access based solely on the merit of the applicant and his/her ability to benefit from undergraduate study.

Yet, while the UK may benefit from greater marketisation within HE, the warts of the US mixed-economy public-private system must be avoided in such a process of Americanisation: 'Higher education is being transformed from a public good to a private commodity, and the very nature and meaning of higher education is narrowing dangerously' (Robert Reich, Brandeis University, quoted in *Times Higher*, 12/3/04). Even so, the risk of such a downside should not mean defaulting to UK HE sinking further into under-resourced Galbraithian public-squalor along the lines of some other European systems. The challenge is to find a sustainable and socially equitable way of funding HE which achieves diversity of access and also allows the best UK HEIs to compete with the US virtual monopoly of world-class universities while at the same time not matching the US in having some of the world's poorest quality HEIs (although, that said, it is not at all clear that the weakest private US HEI is any worse than the least well-resourced public sector HEI in the HE systems of other countries, including the UK).

Moreover, are we anyway seeing divergence or convergence of HE systems, and especially in terms of the balance of funding? If the USA is broadly a mixed-economy, public-private model for the delivery of a national system, and continental Europe a virtual state monopoly with higher education as a public service, is the UK drifting towards one rather than the other, towards Americanisation (marketisation) or towards Europeanisation (as indeed in theory it should be as a member of the EU and given the EU's trajectory towards a degree of HE harmonization by 2010 begun with the Bologna Declaration)? Or might the USA come under pressure to move away from a free market model as its private universities and colleges repeatedly increase tuition fees well above consumer price inflation and even salary inflation? Will politicians in US States demand greater accountability of, and value-for-money from, their public university systems, bringing them closer to the (over)-regulated UK model? And might at least parts of Europe be tempted to shift some of the financial burden from the hard-pressed taxpayer to the student/family by introducing tuition fees, just as, amidst much political acrimony, the Government is proposing to triple tuition fees at English universities from 2006? If thereby the English model is drifting across the Atlantic, might the USA anyway be moving towards it, and might the UK also be towing in its wake the European HE model? Convergence by 2020 in the Azores, or further West in the Bermuda Triangle?

INTRODUCTION
TAXPAYER RETREAT

US and UK Higher Education (HE) have each faced over the past twenty years the steady retreat of the taxpayer in funding students and Higher Education Institutions (HEIs), but, while UK HE has muddled through by accordingly reducing funding per student, US public HE has to a great extent substituted for the lost revenue by increasing tuition fees payable directly by students/their families. US private HEIs have also levied ever-higher tuition fees as 'the sticker-price', and have used the enhanced funding to fuel an arms-race for 'prestige' amongst universities competing on salaries for the best faculty (so-called 'trophy professors'!), on merit-aid for the cleverest students, and on lavish campus infrastructure; and thereby have opened up an increasingly wide gap between themselves and even the 'flagship' US public HEIs, while leaving the best of UK HE aiming at a moving target in trying to compete as a global player.

US public HE is generally less regulated (albeit with wide variations amongst States) than UK HE as 'the last of the nationalised industries', where, ironically, 'regulation' seems to increase as Government funding declines. Moreover, the existence of a flourishing private sector within US HE enhances the whole national HE system's diversity and flexibility, and in turn its overall responsiveness to the needs of the economy and society which it serves. A further paradox is that UK HEIs, while being legally autonomous and hence de jure 'private' in US terms, behave as de facto quasi-public sector entities, and are increasingly treated as such by politicians and civil servants. Yet, despite these high 'sticker-price' tuition fees, US HE remains (just?) affordable for 'Middle America', partly because the US middle-class pays rather less in taxes than its equivalent in the UK and especially given 'deep-discounting' of the tuition fee and the offer of cheap loan money to finance the final amount due (in effect, 'a price-war' amongst US HEIs for clever entrants): and crucially at least 'Rich America' is not being given as much of a wasteful public subsidy as is currently bestowed on 'Rich England' students. These high tuition fees, even with high levels of financial aid, may, however, deter access for 'Poor America' to the very best private US HEIs (and to a lesser extent the best of the public HEIs), compared with the accessibility of the 'elite' UK HEIs.

Hence, if the UK HEIs were completely 'deregulated' with respect to the capping of tuition fees, or chose to exercise their theoretical autonomy and take full control of their destiny, it would be politically wise to have robust policies in place in advance which would ensure at least the same level of accessibility as at present. Oxford, for example, must also be able to demonstrate the financial viability of such access/student financial aid policies as funded (presumably) partly from charging much annual higher tuition fees (£12-15K?) to 'Rich England' and rather higher fees (£7-10K?) to 'Middle England' (taking into account affordability issues), while, of course, charging very little (if anything at all in order to maintain access) to 'Poor England'.

That said, it will be interesting to see if Oxford (and others) could make the 'high fee/high aid' numbers really work, given that, as already noted, it may have a larger 'poor' group to finance than do its overall wealthier US counterparts. In its favour it is probably 'leaner and meaner' in productivity terms than the average US Ivy League: although the contribution towards such economy that comes from the keeping faculty salaries internationally low is a false economy in the mid-term as Oxford increasingly fails to attract for its academic jobs the full range of good applicants and even then does not always manage to recruit its first-choice candidate.

A Hostile Political Environment?

Not, of course, that Oxford, nor 'UK HE plc' generally, receives any credit for this efficiency by OECD norms: instead it gets Mr Lambert's Report for the Treasury on the alleged managerial and governance inefficiency of UK HEIs and, seemingly, Oxford and Cambridge in particular. When the interim report emerged the lead item on the front page of *The Times*, 15/7/03, carried the headline: Oxbridge told to shape or lose freedom – Dithering dons risk world-class status, says Treasury adviser; while the *Financial Times*, 15/7/03, headline read: Oxford and Cambridge 'need sharp business approach'. The Lambert interim document did, however, comment: 'We have found a sector that feels over-scrutinised and distrusted, and is consequently edgy and defensive', a sector over-burdened by 'numerous and uncoordinated initiatives accumulated over many years and without any overarching rationale', and a sector which is 'undercapitalised'. The University of Oxford speedily responded (*Times*, 16/7/03) to the Lambert criticisms by pointing out that world-class universities were not best managed on an analogy with 'a pickle factory', and Alan Ryan (Warden of New College, Oxford) fired off a characteristically incisive newspaper article querying why the same (over-interventionist) Government which had so far so failed to upgrade UK schools and hospitals should now assume it can next successfully 'reform' universities (*Independent*, 24/7/03). The final version of the Lambert Review (www.lambertreview.org.uk) came out in early-December, 2003, again leading to further negative publicity for Oxbridge: for example, the *Financial Times* (5/12/03), 'Oxbridge colleges slated for blocking stance'; and the *Times* (5/12/03), 'Oxbridge gets three year deadline for reform'. If, however, Government concern push comes to bullying shove, for whether the chartered university under modern English Law would be as well protected from the destructive attention of Government as the US private HEIs have been by US Law since the 1819 Dartmouth College case see the OxCHEPS Occasional Paper No. 8 (Palfreyman) at oxcheps.new.ox.ac.uk (also in Education and the Law, 15 (2/3) 149-156, 2003).

The salutary question posed by a hostile political environment for the Oxford Dons currently 'on watch' is whether the potential for accelerated decline relative to the US global players (with their fiercely defended autonomy and robust lobbying of Government) is now so great, and the likelihood of Government 'control freak' meddling intervention being at best useless and at worst damaging, that they must take radical strategic action for fear of otherwise themselves going down in history accountable as the ones who steered the noble 'SS Oxford' onto the rocks, rather than as just (yet) another generation of the University's leadership which 'merely' allowed the unfortunate vessel to drift deeper into the doldrums.

In fact, one college head of house, Lord Butler as Master of University College, has called for tuition fees of at least £5000 – *Sunday Times* 12/10/03. But, if Oxford Dondom generally is in no mood for such boldness, perhaps Oxford might effectively privatise itself on the quiet by trading on its global reputation (while it still has it!) steadily to recruit more overseas students paying high fees and creating space for them by reducing the quantity of Brits for whom nobody (Government-taxpayer, parents-students) is prepared to pay fees at the level necessary to sustain a world-class institution: 'the LSE model', where some 60% of students are higher fee non-UK/EU. In short, UK HE, or at least Oxford and a few others, might now begin to escape from being micro-managed by Government as 'the last nationalised industry', and from being a Welfare State perk for Middle England and even more so for Rich England, by shifting towards the less regressive US HE system's high-fees/high-aid policy. And it just could do so without denting (possibly indeed while widening) accessibility for Poor England, being careful not to let the noisy political protests of the better-off students-families about 'affordability' trump the equity issue of 'access' for low-income students-families (as, sadly, seems to have happened over the past few years in the US).

Follow the US Example? Chasing a moving target?

There is certainly a need in the UK better to understand US HE in the context of the highly politicised debate here about the size, shape and funding of HE as recently fuelled by the Government's White Paper on *The future of higher education* which proposes an increase in tuition fees from £1125 pa to £3000 and which is detailed and discussed in the next chapter, as also is the July 2003 Report of the all-party Education and Skills Committee on 'The Future of Higher Education' which reviews the White Paper and calls for a maximum annual tuition fee of £5000 (as also advocated by the 'top' HEIs) rather than £3000 so as to ensure a true market in the provision of HE. Then chapter 2 explores US HE in broad terms, while chapters 3-5 note that, just as the UK's 'New Labour' Government in its 2003 consultation document sets out 'the need for reform' in terms of shifting the cost of HE more towards students and their families, so there has been debate in the USA over the cost/accountability and affordability/accessibility of HE since Congress in 1997 expressed the frustration of 'Middle America' with the ever-increasing 'cost of college' by establishing the National Commission on the Cost of Higher Education. Yet, despite the middle-class angst, an observer of the HE scene across the OECD countries might indeed be tempted to predict a slow but steady convergence towards the US norm of requiring an increasingly significant student/family contribution towards the cost of delivering HE: the 'Americanisation' of HE funding across all OECD countries.

The White Paper proposed £3K pa fee from 2006 would take the current £3300 figure over the standard three-year undergraduate degree course (and paid in full anyway by only some 40% of UK students) to £9K (c$14K compared with, by then, for the four-year baccalaureate c$20/25K at the US public HEIs, and perhaps $30K-plus at the research-oriented flagship campus within each State HE system...): thus, the White Paper is indeed aiming at a moving target in trying to keep the upper end of UK HEIs competitive in income terms with even the best of the US publics, let alone the top private HEIs where annual fees are already exceeding $30K. And, indeed there is also a trend towards the semi-privatisation of the State flagship campus institutions (now being called 'the public Ivies'!), which may push fees yet higher than the c$7K pa referred to above.

8

If UK and US HE may well continue to diverge on funding, they will then share certain features in that the politics of affordability of HE for 'Middle America' have during the 1990s trumped the politics of access to HE for 'Poor America', which is not surprising given the relative voting power of the two constituencies: a scenario potentially to be echoed in the UK, where in response to New Labour's White Paper and its proposed £3K pa tuition fee for 'Middle England', the Conservative Party has focussed on affordability, asserting at one point that it would avoid the need to increase fees (or even levying them at all) by reducing the size of the HE system and hence its accessibility to 'Poor England' as a means of saving money.

A Strategy Vacuum?

Yet, given the harsh reality of 'the politics of HE' and the voting power of the better-off, the White Paper proposals may yet run into the sand, leaving a strategy vacuum that the HEIs then fail to fill since they them-selves are split as their leaders (the Vice-Chancellors gathered at Universities UK as 'the trade body') squabble over whether the tuition fee cap should be set at an almost worthwhile £5K pa (the figure favoured by the 'Russell Group' of the 'top' 15-20 universities), at the White Paper's proposed modest £3K (as acceptable to perhaps most HEIs), at a £2K 'quick-fix' and somewhat defeatist compromise (as floated by one promi-nent VC), at a strictly non-variable level of £2,500 (as proposed by 15 VCs in a letter to the *Guardian* , or at the present meagre £1125 (as dreamt of by those few VCs hanging on to the fantasy of HE being one day once again adequately funded by the taxpayer. They are joined in their naivety by the major HE unions who, even post-'massification' within HE, still cling to the tempting idea but anachronistic ideal of all HEIs being the same in purpose and hence to be funded equally (although the University of Nottingham Students' Union has displayed greater common-sense, its President declaring: 'You have to be realistic. We feel they [fees] are an inevitability. We believe it's better to try and get the best deal possible.' – *Guardian*, 6/4/04). The only consolation in observing such dissension within the ranks of UUK is that it might, at long last, herald the collapse of this weak lobby-group ('a hotbed of cold-feet' as one former VC famously commented, and one noted for 'its habit of pre-emptive surren-der' according to Alan Ryan, *Times Higher*, 26/9/03, p17: see also the trenchant criticism by Simon Jenkins in *Times*, 15/10/03) as it becomes abundantly clear that such an unwieldy grouping is not able properly to represent the increasingly diverse interests of so many HEIs and their different missions within, and differing contributions to, the delivery of HE in this country.

Whether, however, Oxford, Cambridge, UCL, Imperial and LSE could fill that strategic vacuum by themselves displaying robust and imaginative leadership to, and for, the whole sector would (some might say) be as uncharacteristic as it may be both vitally necessary for, and also even grudgingly or more likely silently welcomed by, the rest of the sector... In short, as Martin Wolf, a *Financial Times* journalist justly celebrated for his acute and perceptive observation of UK HE, has commented (*Financial Times*, 3/10/03, p 21): 'If the UK does not find a way to increase resources going to universities substantially, free them from excessive control and sustain a number of institutions that match the best the US has to offer, it will betray its future. The education it provides may be 'free', but it will be in the mediocre institutions of an intellectually irrelevant country. This need not happen. But it looks increasingly probable. Parliament should dare to choose a better outcome.' (See also Wolf's neat and convincing Paper, 'How to save the British universities', 26/9/02, at www. sfim.co.uk/pdfs/Universities_Lecture.pdf.)

Wolf's fellow *FT* columnist, John Kay, makes the case for increased marketisation within UK, and indeed European, HE (7/1/04): 'We shall have better education and fairer access if government money is directed to students, not colleges. With state funding of universities comes state control of universities. This has been disastrous. Government has not been successful at managing banks, airlines or even railways. It is even worse at directing universities, which are by nature pluralist institutions...and fit badly into risk-averse and centralised bureaucratic systems of control.' Kay points to the US monopoly of world class HEIs, and to most of those being 'the triumph of autonomous institutions over government-controlled ones'. Thus, 'Harvard and Chicago, Princeton and Caltech do not negotiate policies with any government agency...These institutions are vacuuming up talent from around the world. Maybe Europe can just let this happen. But it is a big risk to take.'

1

UK HIGHER EDUCATION
THE 2003 WHITE PAPER

This book explores the economics of delivering UK and US higher education (HE) as a system and at the level of the individual higher education institution (HEI):

- What does HE cost in terms of Government financial support to HEIs and also by way of grants/loans to students, and what does the undergraduate degree cost the HEI to deliver?
- How does the US HEI decide 'the sticker-price' fee for the undergraduate degree course and determine the extent to which it will then discount that annual tuition fee via packages of its own financial aid awarded to particular students?
- How affordable, as discounted through such needs-blind admission or merit-aid, is US HE, in both public and private HEIs, for 'Middle America'?
- How accessible, given Federal/State grants/loans and also HEI financial aid, is US HE, at both public and private HEIs, for 'Poor America'?
- To what extent both in the UK and in the US have those paying for HE, the politicians on behalf of the taxpayer's subsidy of the public HEIs and the students/their families personally footing the bill via increasing tuition fees, demanded greater accountability from HEIs in terms of value-for-money?

The White Paper

There is a need better to understand US HE in the context of the highly politicised debate in the UK about the size, shape and funding of HE as recently fuelled by the Government's White Paper on *The future of higher education* (Cm 5735, 2003, London: The Stationery Office), which is concerned with:

- Enhancing the funding of HE and HEIs so as to allow them 'to compete with the world's best' and to avoid the 'serious risk of decline' after 'decades of under-investment' (notably, as UK HE by

OECD norms rather belatedly massified, 'Funding per student fell by 36 per cent between 1989 and 1997').

- Ensuring the affordability for 'Middle England' of the proposed increase of the current flat-rate £1125 (c$1700:NB £-$ at 1.00-1.50 for all comparisons given) annual tuition fee to one capped at £3000 (c$4500) from 2006 by 'abolishing up-front tuition fees for all students' and with their repayment after graduation through the tax system then being 'linked to ability to pay'.

- Extending the availability of HE 'to the talented and best from all backgrounds' and improving its accessibility for 'less advantaged families', given that 'The social class gap among those entering university remains too wide' (and indeed has 'widened', something which 'cannot be tolerated in a civilised society' and which 'is inherently socially unjust') and given that 'Young people from professional [family] backgrounds are over five times more likely to enter higher education than those from unskilled backgrounds'. (See below for data on the 'access' issue within UK HE.)

- Developing Government financial aid for such students from 'less advantaged families' ('those who come from the poorest backgrounds should get extra support'). (See below for detail of current levels of Government financial aid to students in UK HE.)

The 2003 White Paper can be viewed at the Department for Education and Science web-site, www.dfes.gov.uk/highereducation. The transcript of an interesting Congration debate on 'University Funding and Fees' held within the University of Oxford can be read at www.ox.ac.uk/gazette/2002-03/supps/4-65655.htm. See also the Oxford Vice-Chancellor's 2003/04 Oration in the *Gazette*, No. 4671 (pp 129-135). The July 2003 Report of the all-party Education and Skills Committee on 'The Future of Higher Education' (HC 425-1) reviews the White Paper and calls for a maximum annual tuition fee of £5000 ($7500) rather than £3000 ($4500) so as to ensure a true market in the provision of HE; it can readily be seen in full at www.parliament.uk/parliamentary-committees/education-and-skills-committee.cfm. The Report fears that 'too great a reliance on funding through taxation will inevitably lead to greater Government control of the sector and less independence for universities', assesses the proposed 'Access Regulator' as 'unnecessary', regards the creation of 'Foundation Degrees' as a means of hitting the 'arbitrarily chosen' 50% target as 'unwise', suggests £5000 ($7500) pa maintenance grants, brands the present student financial aid system as 'complex and confusing', and comments that academic salaries are 'woefully low'. UUK (universitiesuk.ac) has also published some useful material: the 'Final Report of the Funding Options Review Group' (Taylor) identifies the shortfall in the funding of teaching at c£600m pa, a figure *not* including extra pay for academics or capital needs and one which equates to charging undergraduates about an extra £700 pa; while the three reports on the 'Pattern of higher education institutions in the UK' (Ramsden, 2001/2002/2003) provide a wealth of data on 'UK HE plc' as roughly a £12b economic activity educating some 2m students in about 165 HEIs (and where 1 in 8 students pay tuition fees at the overseas rate, bringing in c£750m pa); see also 'Achieving our Vision'.

The Government has quickly brushed off the carefully researched Report of the Select Committee and is sticking with its rather less evidence-based White Paper, which seems sadly to achieve the worst of all worlds by maximising opposition (uniting in terms of HE policy-making the National Union of Students, the Lib-Dems, and Old Labour (reinforced by those New Labour MPs fearful of their re-election prospects in marginal Middle England constituencies) with the Tory front bench and also with the anti-Blair *Daily Mail* in defending Middle England's right to Welfare State free(ish) HE) and yet at the same time watering down the degree of proposed deregulation to such an extent that the £3000 fee (allowed to increase by only inflation until 2012 or so) will be of no real value in enabling UK HE 'to compete with the world's best'. And anyway it will come with such strings attached as to make it barely worth any self-respecting HEI dancing on the end of them for the resultant paltry financial gain.

Indeed, the prospect for UK HE could well be twenty years of detrimental political intervention, commencing with the policy-making chaos following the receipt of the damp-squib 1997 Dearing Report clumsily yielding the minimalist £1000 flat-rate tuition fee, then the intellectual poverty of the 2003 White Paper generating by 2006 the introduction of the already obviously inadequate £3000 maximum fee, and hence leaving the whole issue of whether at least part of the UK's HE system is to be adequately financed to match the better US HEIs to be fought through yet again around 2010 and with little chance of realistic fee levels being fully phased in until 2015 or so. By then (2015/2020) UK HE can safely have been written off as a serious global player, leaving the US a clean sweep of the world's best HEIs and the children or grand-children of today's politicians, opinion-formers and chattering-classes no doubt jumping ship and safely securing for themselves comfortable billets by studying at an American Ivy League or at what by then could be a range of almost as well-resourced American semi-privatised flagship public HEIs! Indeed, the children of the upper echelons of German and Austrian society already escape the over-crowded and under-resourced mediocrity of their mass national HE systems by fleeing to the US, and (for now) also even to the upper end of the UK system, and in fact increasingly to the recently created private HEIs (as in Italy and some former Eastern European countries).

Rates of Return

Moreover, since the White Paper emerged, there have been a number of DfEE-sponsored studies attempting, inter alia, to calculate the private rate of return on completing HE. This is a vexed issue involving simplistic headlines of £400K ($600K) over a lifetime, but where there is (or, rather, was!) some convergence on 11/14% - incidentally, remarkably similar to the US figures. See Reports 7 & 8 of *Higher Education in the learning society* (The National Committee of Inquiry into Higher Education, 1997, London: HMSO; aka 'The Dearing Report'). A September 2003 OECD Report (*Education at a Glance*), however, puts the private rate of return for UK HE at 17% for men and 15% for women (the highest rates of any OECD country), with 37% of young people graduating (against an OECD average of 30%) – this figure of 37% being helped by the UK's low drop-out rate (less than 20% compared with, say, 40% in France and even higher in Italy - see chapter 3 for US data). These 17/15% figures are boosted by the fact that State financial aid to UK students is relatively generous and hence students incur less debt, and also by UK degrees being only 3 or 4 years compared with OECD norms of 4/5 and hence the UK graduate has a longer earning period. Not surprisingly the Government has quickly latched on to this data as strongly supporting its push for higher tuition fees! (Sadly, the same OECD Report is rather less positive about UK schooling, where, arguably any extra public spending might be better used than in HE.) The Report also comments that the UK spent in 2000 only 1% of GDP on HE, leaving it 20th within 29 OECD countries and falling from 10th at 1.2% in 1995: the 2000 OECD average was 1.3%; the US tips in at 2.7%, given its willingness to allow a private (student/family) input via tuition fees which effectively doubles the public spend.

Yet note the increasing uncertainty over whether high graduate output from mass HE could mean poorer earnings potential and hence a lower rate of personal return for more recent generations of graduates (for example, the personal rate of return may be falling according to one study: Mason, G. (2002) 'High skills utilisation under mass higher education: graduate employment in service industries in Britain', in Journal of

Education and Work 15 (4) 427-456); or it may be increasing to over 16% as calculated by Peter Elias (University of Warwick) and Kate Purcell (University of West of England) for a Higher Education Policy Institute Seminar in September 2003.); see also the thorough HEPI Report on 'Demand for Graduates: A Review of Economic Evidence', at the 'Articles' Page of *www.hepi.ac.uk*, along with Gemmell, N. (1997) Report 8 of the Dearing Report on 'Externalities to Higher Education: a Review of the New Growth Literature'.)

In essence, there is no conclusive evidence that expanding HE will alone improve economic performance by providing *high-skills* employees (as argued in the so-called 'New Growth Theories' and their assumptions about human capital as economic inputs). So, rich nations are not necessarily rich because they have mass HE systems; they may become wealthy first and only then can afford mass HE as 'a luxury good' for their youth. The same taxpayer cash spent on expanding HE may well be better spent in FE or in schools or in, say, improving transport, in terms of adding to economic productivity and promoting economic growth.

This, of course, is not to say that there is not a social or cultural or a citizenship, or even a political, case for expanding HE. Nor does this mean that expansion of HE via the cheap route of the proposed 2-year 'Foundation Degrees' in vocational subjects would not be valuable in terms of filling an *intermediate-skills* gap in the economy. Similarly, spending on research and intellectual property exploitation within HE may also benefit the economy (see Porter, M. (2003), 'UK Competitiveness', DTi Economics Paper No. 3 at *www.dti.gov.uk* – 'Publications' via the 'Site Index', then 'Economics').

Referring back to the HEPI Report cited above, that Report notes that the private rate of return to a degree is 'considerably higher' than the social rate of return, and that such 'uneven benefits to the individual and to society' support Government proposals to increase tuition fees. The Report finds that the purely economic case for expanding HE is weak compared with the 'very strong non-economic arguments', and that Government's embracing of New Growth Theories as its utilitarian justification for HE expansion may 'lead to wasted resources and disappointed expectations' unless other steps are taken to ensure that the increased supply of graduates within the labour force can be properly and fully utilised. (See also Alison Wolf's book as cited below which explores 'myths about education and economic growth' (awkward reading for those in 'the HE industry'!), and related papers on the demand for HE at the HEPI web-site.)

So, whether barely 10% or above 15% for the private rate of return (cf c 10% for the social rate of return), HE generally (and at least hitherto) is a good personal investment, but one of these more recent analyses (Chevalier & Conlon, 'Does it pay to attend a prestigious university?' (March 2003) LSE: Centre for the Economics of Education *http://cee.lse.ac.uk/publications.htm*) goes further and answers in the affirmative the question posed in the title of the study: 'It seems that the human capital of graduates is permanently increased by graduating from a prestigious institution' (p 17). The Paper's conclusions are, of course, again helpful for those hoping that, post-2006, such 'prestigious' HEIs (in effect 'the Russell Group') will indeed take the opportunity of the proposed semi-deregulation to charge the full £3000 pa 'permitted'* as the capped tuition fee, and to defend doing so on the basis that the Paper finds that the earnings premium for the (male) graduate of the 'elite' HEI is 6% pa over his counterpart from 'a Modern university'. The authors suggest this would justify a fee premium of between £3K and £7K pa for top UK HEIs in order to correct partially the Government's 'inequitable policy' of currently subsidising students 'attending prestigious universities more generously than others'. Interestingly, no such earnings premium is found for 'non-Russell Group' chartered/'old' HEIs over the ex-polytechnic 'Modern' ones. The reason for the premium is asserted to be 'better quality teaching' (linked to the academics in these HEIs being research-active?) rather than solely 'a network effect' or a 'signalling' effect of concentrating largely middle-class students in such HEIs. The study notes that 'our calculations are also in line with US evidence, where the providers of higher education are free to set their price' (p 18).

In contrast to Chevelier & Conlon, P. Brown (Cardiff University) & A. Hesketh (Lancaster University) suggest (September, 2003; see also their *The Mismanagement of Talent*, OUP, 2004 forthcoming) that 'good graduate jobs' go to 'an elite' of graduates from the top HEIs, to those young people combining such 'elite credentials' with distinctive 'personal' qualities and a 'cosmopolitan' status (say, extensive and interesting travel in a 'gap-year') associated with the social and cultural capital of a secure middle-class upbringing. The Council for Industry and Education (CIHE), however, in its October 2003 'The Value of Higher Education' (CIHE@btinternet.com), is more upbeat about there being jobs, at least of some kind, for all graduates and about UK HE needing to expand – and the CIHE supports the White Paper's proposed higher and variable tuition fees.

* Where the word 'permitted' is used above, it is in '' marks because, as it is significant to note, all UK HEIs are legally autonomous charitable cor-

porations, whether chartered or statutory, and hence the Government is not, technically, able to prevent them charging any level of tuition fee they wish. The fact that UK HE behaves as if it is 'the last nationalised industry' while Government pays even less of the cost of HE but calls ever more of the tune does not alter the legal reality that, if a university broke ranks by charging above the cap on tuition fees, the Government's only immediate revenge could be to consider exercising the power it has given itself to request/instruct HEFCE to reduce £ for £ that institution's public money block-grant. It is unclear, however, whether Government ire would extend beyond the teaching component of the HEFCE block-grant and cut into the element awarded for research productivity, especially if the HEI concerned, despite higher fees, was careful somehow to protect accessibility for students from lower socio-economic groups...See Palfreyman & Warner, *Higher Education Law*, 2002 (Bristol: Jordans), chapter 2, on the legal status of an English HEI; and OxCHEPS Paper No. 8 (Palfreyman) on its legal vulnerability to Government 'reform', at oxcheps.new.ox.ac.uk (also in *Education and the Law*, 2003, vol.16 issue 2/3).

Will £3K be enough?

Thus, since 'the world's best' HEIs are mainly to be found in the USA and since the US HE system charges rather higher tuition fees over the years of the typical 4-year Liberal Arts first degree, certainly at the private HEIs but also increasingly at the public HEIs (and especially at the 'flagship' State HEIs, such as in Berkeley, Michigan, Texas and Virginia), than the £3K pa for the typical 3-year single honours degree UK HEIs may be 'allowed' to levy from 2006 (let alone the modest £1125 currently charged in 2003/04), there are clearly interesting questions as to how those top US HEIs fund their academic pre-eminence and also how students finance their studies at them or indeed elsewhere in the US HE system. Will £3K from 2006 really provide the extra resources for UK HE to compete with the best? How effective is US HE, with high fees helping to fund that high international status, at balancing reasonable affordability for 'Middle America' with appropriate levels of access for 'Poor America'? Are there lessons to be learnt from the US experience as UK HE seems on the verge of moving closer to the US mixed-economy model and further away from the 'free public good' economy of EU HE systems? (See John Douglass, 'Is California's higher education system a model for UK HE?' in *Perspectives* (7, 2, 2003; pp 41-47), as also available at the OxCHEPS web-site under 'Papers'-'Conference Proceedings'.)

Or might we see steady convergence amongst OECD HE systems generally on the US public/private model? Private HEIs, as noted earlier, are springing up, for example, in Italy, in Austria, in some former Eastern Bloc European nations, and in several Latin America countries, while Japan seems about to partially-deregulate and semi-privatise all its one hundred or so 'national' universities. In the UK all HEIs are already de jure 'private' in the terms of the US 1819 Dartmouth College case, but, in practice, such is their (albeit declining) dependency on Government funding combined with their poor strategic vision, only the tiny University of Buckingham behaves in a truly autonomous way along US small Liberal Arts college lines: the rest de facto constitute UK HE as 'the last nationalised industry'!

UK Access Data

Report 6 of 'The Dearing Report' considers the issue of 'widening participation in higher education by students from lower socio-economic groups...' (SEGs), and thereby provides the most readily accessible analysis and discussion of access data for UK HE. Further material on access can, however, be found on the OxCHEPS web-site at 'Bibliography' – 'Access' and on the 'Statistics' page; see also Tapper & Palfreyman (forthcoming, Falmer Routledge / Taylor & Francis 2004), *Understanding Mass Higher Education: Comparative Perspectives on Access*, and, specifically on the UK, three recent books: Archer, L., Hutchings, M. & Ross, A. (2003) *Can higher education ever be truly inclusive?: issues of exclusion and inclusion.* London: Routledge; Hayton, A. & Paczuska, A. (2002) *Access, participation and higher education: policy and practice.* London: Kogan Page; and Power, S., et al (2003) *Education and the middle class.* Buckingham: Open University Press. There are also valuable and well-presented access data in a Report on 'Widening Participation and Fair Access' at the 'Articles' Page of the HEPI web-site at *www.hepi.ac.uk*.

Report 6 discusses 'the problem of under-representation' within HE of lower socio-economic groups, seeing it as 'a reasonable cause for public concern' (a theme picked up in the 2003 White Paper). In the context of the 'massification' of UK HE and a doubling of the overall API to c35% over the last 15 years (Table 1 of the Report, p 37; as updated to 2002), the API of SEGs I/II/IIIn 18 year-olds had reached 45% by 1995 in contrast to 15% for SEGs IIIm/IV/V: a ratio of 3 to 1 (cf 1950, 18%:3%, 6:1; 1970, 32%:5%, 6:1) (Table 1.1, p 40). More starkly, the API for SEG I at 80% plays 12% for SEG V (Table 1.2, p 40). Thus, the access data seems to show rather 'slow improvement for lower socio-economic participation'.

Moreover, even if the lower SEG 18 year-olds reach HE, they are more likely to be 'in lower status courses at lower status institutions' and also less likely to graduate than their SEG I & II counterparts; still less will they get 'top' graduate jobs assuming they do graduate: paras 1.11 & 12; see also Patrick Ainley, *Degrees of Difference: Higher Education in the 1990s* (1994, London: Lawrence & Wishart) and Anthony Giddens, *The Class Structure of Advanced Societies* (1973, London: Hutchinson), along with an Open University 2004 Report, 'Access to What?' (OU Centre for HE Research, J. Brannan). The end result is that the SEG I child is 4x more likely, and the SEG V child 3x less likely, 'to obtain a first degree than their proportion in the population would suggest' (para. 2.17). That said, Report 6 comments that there may be room for a 'more optimistic inter-pretation' in that the trend for participation by lower SEGs 'seems to have broken out of the historic range'.

Similarly, another ready source of data, and of perceptive analysis, on the access issue is Alison Wolf, *Does Education Matter? - myths about educa-tion and economic growth* (2002, London: Penquin; especially pp 187-199). On page 192, for example, Wolf records 'the family origins of UK stu-dents' as a %age of total fresher undergraduates coming from each of the SEGs: I/II/IIIn provided 74% of the students in 1960, and, 40 years on, they still supply exactly 74%; the supply from SEGs IV &V increased over this time from 7% to 9%. (On p 283 the %age of 'eighteen-year-olds by social class of birth family' for 2000 is given as 55% for SEGs IV & V, and 34% for SEGs I & II.) Later she gives the US figures (p 195), showing for 1992 the bottom 25% family income group having half its 'young people entering college' compared with over 90% from the top quartile of earners. While US HE seems, therefore, generally to score better on access, just as in the UK the 'poor' are, however, diverted into certain HEIs: in 1997 a mere 1% of students at 'highly selective private universities' were from the 'low-income' groups compared with 11% from the 'richest'; in the 'highly selective public universities' the corresponding figures were 3% and 9%; and in the community colleges (offering the US equivalent of the White Paper's proposed 'Foundation Degrees') the figures were 47% and 12%. But, while access to the best resourced elements of HE is skewed in favour of the rich in both countries, at least in the case of the US rich kids attending the top private HEIs they receive no public subsidy and, indeed, since such private HEIs are seemingly islands of social redistrib-ution/engineering within a generally conservative (by European stan-dards) political system, they are also paying hefty tuition fees which help to subsidise affordability for middle-income families and (to a lesser extent?) access for lower income families! (For more on the US data see the 'Affordability' and 'Access' chapters below.)

Wolf provides comparator data for the UK HEIs (p 213): in 1998 80% of Cambridge students were from SEGs I & II, while at Leeds it was 69%, at Thames Valley 33% and at the University of Central Lancashire a mere 21%. Archer et al, as referred to above, give figures for the '% of group starting HE', dividing the under-21 cohort according to SEG: I, 90%; II, 55%; IIInm, 20%; IIIm, 10%; IV, 10%; V, 5% (p 78). Recent HEFCE data gives the most 'middle-class' HEIs as Cambridge (91% from social classes A, B, C1), along with others above 85% such as Oxford, Bristol, Durham, Nottingham, Imperial, UCL and Warwick; all of these are, of course, also the ones with the lowest drop-out rates (2-6%), with some of the lowest State school intakes (Oxford at 53%, UCL 60%, Durham 62.5%), with the highest A-level entry scores (Oxford at 29.5 against a theoretical maximum of 30 points for 3 'A's, Imperial 28.1, Warwick 26.6, UCL 25.7), awarding the most 1sts and 2.1s (Cambridge at 89%, Bristol 82%, Nottingham 76%), having the best QAA scores (Cambridge at 96%, Imperial 82%, Warwick 74%), with the best staff-student ratios (UCL at 7.33, Bristol 10.87), having the fewest students from deprived areas (Bristol at 4.5%, Oxford 5.5%), and with the top RAE scores (Cambridge at 92.5%, Oxford 89%, Warwick 80.5%, UCL 78%). The most 'working-class' HEIs (Wolverhampton with 47.5% from C2/D/E, Luton and Greenwich both at 39%) are the mirror-image of the above cluster of seven in almost every respect: for example, Luton's 9.0 A-level points is the lowest in the sector (the other two are both at 11.6); Wolverhampton has 98.5% State school entrants and 23.5% from deprived areas; the Greenwich SSR is 23.29; Luton gets 9% for research; Wolverhampton is awarded 37.5% for its teaching; and so on... Thus, the *Sunday Times* 'University Guide' (2003) puts our middle-class seven firmly in the top ten, while our working-class three tip in at 89, 83 and 111 within the 121 UK HEIs. And still some Labour MPs, opposing the White Paper's proposals for variable tuition fees amongst HEIs, talk as if there does not already exist a two (or, in fact, a multi-) tier HE system in the UK; indeed, as Peter Knight (Vice-Chancellor, University of Central England), writes welcoming the principle of variable top-up fees (*Education Guardian*, 13/1/04): 'Where have you been for the last 20 years? The system has more tiers in it than I can count...'

It is difficult, however, to see how such a skewing is avoidable, short of elite UK HE introducing distinctly 'affirmative action' admission policies or Government tackling deep deficiencies in State schooling, given that SEG I is 8% of the population but provides 36% of the HE applicants with the top 3 Grade As at 'A'-level ('A'-levels at age 18 being the UK equivalent of US High School graduation and SAT entry to HE) and that the usual entry score for Oxbridge is at least AAB: SEG II figures are 21% and 43%, SEG IIIn 19% and 9%, SEG IIIm 33% and 8.5%, SEG IV 14% and 3%, SEG V 5% and 0.6%   (The data for the supposedly egalitarian French 'open access' HE system looks even worse (p 210 of Wolf): 1% of students at the Ecole Nationale d'Administration in 1978/82 were from a 'workers and artisans' background, as opposed to the 19% as the children of 'senior civil servants' (clearly, a matter of genetics!) and the 15% from the 'professions'.)

All in all, then, it is difficult to disagree with Nicholas Barr (*The Welfare State as Piggy Bank*, 2001, Oxford: OUP), who concludes that UK HE remains a public service 'disproportionately consumed by people from better off backgrounds' (p 180) and hence for which the substantial 'taxpayer subsidies are regressive: the taxes of truck-drivers pay for the degrees of old Etonians' (p 216). Similarly, Niall Ferguson (*The Cash Nexus: Money and Power in the Modern World, 1700-2000*, 2001, London: Penquin) comments (p 211/212): 'Even more perversely, the bulk of benefits under the universal welfare system... flows not to the poor but to the rich... the wealthiest fifth of the UK population receive 40 per cent more public spending on health than the poorest fifth; with respect to secondary education the figure is 80 per cent, to university education 500 per cent...'!

A. H. Halsey (*Decline of Donnish Dominion*, 1992, Oxford: OUP, pp 102/103) notes 'the general tendency for inequality of education attainment to persist in relative terms' amongst social classes, along with 'an important cross-national hypothesis which awaits rigorous test – that [HE] expansion in the post-war period has been accommodated by a pattern of [HEI] institutional development...such that the most prestigious universities (the Harvards and Stanfords in the USA, the Grandes Ecoles in France, the ex-Imperial universities in Japan) have actually narrowed their recruitment on to the upper echelons of the professional, managerial, and bourgeois classes'. Halsey sees 'the possibility of this particular form of social polarization' as 'the nightmare of an educationally polarized society', warning that, while 'the evidence of polarization so far is inconclusive', 'the movement [in UK HE] from grants towards loans inaugurated in 1989 [and reinforced by the abolition of grants by New Labour in 1997?] and the logic of education as a positional good might well produce greater class inequality in British higher education in the future.'

Finally, Peter Scott provides an astute and pithy snapshot of UK HE in 2001 (in *The State of UK Higher Education: Managing Change and Diversity*, Warner &

Palfreyman, Buckingham: Open University Press, p 193): '...two broad messages are plain. First, although the number of students has tripled during the past three decades, there has been only a limited shift in the composition of the student body. British higher education has become a mass system because participation rates among the spreading middle class are now 'universal' (in Trow's terminology) while among the working class access to higher education has remained an 'elite' experience confined to the academically able and the highly motivated. Second, working-class students are heavily concentrated in less prestigious institutions. The student mix in elite universities has changed remarkably little since the 'golden time' of the 1960s; to the extent that the system has become more open it has been because of the addition of new institutions with wider constituencies...'

Here, it should be noted, we are concerned with 'access' as a SEG issue (see below* for the definition of the SEGs); there are, of course, also other dimensions to the access debate involving participation in HE by ethnic minorities (a major political concern for US HE, and especially as a Supreme Court decision has just given a partial victory for the challenge against 'affirmative action' admission policies), by the disabled, and – to a lesser extent as 'a problem' now largely addressed in the 'mass' UK HE system of the 2000s – by women: see Report 5 of 'The Dearing Report'. Moreover, it is, of course, very difficult, as will be discussed in the 'Access' section below, to compare UK data based on SEGs with US data largely focusing on income and ethnicity: the child of the Oxford Don attending Cambridge would be yet another SEG I student and hence not claimable as progress in the name of 'widening access'; but, in the unlikely event of Dad the Don getting an academic job at Yale on the same (lowish) salary as at Oxford the child then attending Harvard would be from merely a middling US income group and, presumably, Harvard would claim it was achieving some social mobility and accessibility!)

* The SEGs are: I, Professional (doctors, dentists, lawyers, engineers, accountants, university lecturers, etc); II, Managerial & Technical (general managers, local government officers, social workers, school-teachers, nurses, etc); III NM, Skilled – non-manual (clerks, cashiers, secretaries, etc); III M, Skilled – manual (electricians, plumbers, car mechanics, carpenters, etc); IV, Partly-Skilled (machinists, security personnel, waiters, etc); V, Unskilled (miners, bus drivers, train staff, production line/factory workers, labourers, etc). Clearly, the overlap of high/low SEG with high/low income band is not perfect (and why should it be?), in that, for example, the SEG III M competent self-employed plumber in London will

probably earn more than the SEG I Oxford Don or SEG II Manchester teacher or nurse but certainly not as much as the SEG I City lawyer or SEG II director of a sizeable company, leaving us with some difficulty in assuming any meaningful matching of student SEGs with student family wealth (the 80% SEGs I & II students at Cambridge are surely not all from London lawyer wealthy families!) and again in accurately comparing UK HEI admissions data with US HEI admissions data for purposes of predicting how many UK students could really afford to pay the full amount of much higher tuition fees and how many would genuinely need 'the sticker-price' discounted by varying amounts through the HEI's offer of financial aid. UK HEIs just do not have access to the family income data that their US counterparts routinely see as part of the admissions process; the nearest they get is knowing, at or after matriculation, that the LEA means-testing mechanism has determined on the basis of family income that the flat-rate tuition fee will be payable by the student in full, in part or not at all and that he/she can claim the full SLC loan or a reduced loan. Otherwise, at the time of application/admission the UK HEI has only post-code (US zip-code) data, giving some clue to family wealth (see Appendix 3).

UK Government Financial Aid to Students

As UK HE has (belatedly by OECD norms) become a 'mass' system, the Government has controlled its cost to the taxpayer by shifting from relatively generous (again by OECD norms) financial aid, means-tested against parental annual income and awarded as 'the student grant' (together with the general subsidy of HE costs via grants direct to HEIs and with no charging of tuition fees to students), to 'the student loan' (together with the continuation (albeit at a reduced level per student) of Government funding direct to HEIs; but with the introduction of a flat-rate annual tuition fee of £1000 ($1500) in 1998/99 (£1125 by 2003), also means-tested). This £1000 applied only to UK/EU undergraduate full-time students; non-UK/EU students already paid 'overseas' fees at 'the economic cost' at (2002/03 figures) some £7500 ($11250) pa for arts/social studies subjects, £10K ($15K) for the sciences, and £18K ($27K) for medicine (a differentiation similar to the US 'in-state'/'out-of-state' fee bands at the public HEIs). Some 60% of UK undergraduate students are, however, exempted from paying fees in full or in part.

It is this RPI-linked 1998 £1000 that the 2003 White Paper proposes should become £3000 from 2006 for that year's new students. The means-testing currently provides full fees exemption, a grant of up to £1000 pa,

and a full student loan of c£4000 pa (less if living at home, more if study-
ing away from home at a London HEI) where family income is up to
c£20K (very roughly the average wage in the UK is £24.5K - $38K); the
grant ends at just above the £20K; between £20K and £30K the fees gradually become payable in full, and the maximum available loan is also
steadily reduced to £3000; the loan carries a taxpayer-subsidised rate of
interest at RPI (say, 2.5%) and becomes repayable once the graduate is
earning c£15K pa (at £15 per month; £75 pm at £20K pa): hence an element
of the frenzied haggling over the content of the 2004 Bill arising from the
2003 White Paper has been whether the £15K threshold should be raised
to £20K. There is additional financial aid for students with disabilities,
with children, from deprived areas; and there is some extra help for those
facing financial hardship because of illness, sudden parental unemployment, and other unforeseeable difficulties. In addition, there is a trend for
some UK HEIs to create US-style 'access bursaries' (the University of
Cambridge, for example, is talking of £4K where a student's family
income is £15K or less, as also is Imperial).

The White Paper proposals do not affect these fee remission, grant and
loan arrangements; but will add a further loan of between £1850 and
£3000 pa so that no student need find the newly-raised annual tuition fee
from his/her own (or parents') resources where his/her chosen HEI has
decided to levy the £3000 maximum amount and where fee remission of
up to £1125 is not already applicable because the family income exceeds
the £20K. Clearly, this extra loan capacity helps affordability for lower-
middle and middle-middle England, but is further unnecessary and
wasteful subsidy for higher income groups. In essence, however, the loan
is clearly inadequate (in US terms, leaving 'unmet need': see chapter 2) at
some £4500 max for meeting the c£6K annual cost of living as a student
away from home (and it is especially inadequate for the student whose
family income exceeds £20K and who then becomes fully liable at £30K
for the current maximum annual tuition fees at the £1125 flat rate). Hence
the UK 1990s student financial aid system implicitly assumes parental
help, earnings from term-time/vacation employment, other sources of
borrowing such as bank overdrafts, etc.

This is in contrast to, say, the author's experience in the early-1970s
when, as the product of a SEG IIIn average-wage Mancunian family, a
nearly full grant (£430 of £460 pa – worth some £3750 in 2003 £s) was
indeed adequate, along with the LEA also paying all my Oxford tuition
fees and travel costs to/from/within Oxford, my finding some vacation
work (or 'signing-on' for unemployment benefit as was still possible for
students in vacations), and having kind parental support by way of free

room-and-board in vacations, to provide a debt-free route through HE (of course, back then students did not have to fund a mobile 'phone habit, and going to the pub/college-student union bar was cheaper than 'club-bing' on 'alcolpops'!). Chances are that, in trying to get the White Paper proposals through Parliament, the Government will make concessions over the level of student financial aid.

In Scotland since Devolution, and in Wales since quasi-devolution, the Cubie Report (1999) and the Rees Report (2001) have, respectively, sought to shift towards the payment of tuition fees not being required 'up-front' but being (re)paid after graduation; the 2003 White Paper proposes essentially the same for England from 2006.

The 2004 Higher Education Bill

The final student tuition fees and financial aid package that emerged as the 2003 White Paper turned into the Higher Education Bill early in 2004 is as follows: the proposed variable annual tuition fees of up to £3K will not be paid up-front by the student, but repaid after graduation and once earning £15K pa, with any remaining debt written-off at the end of 25 years; HEIs levying the full fee are to provide a £300 bursary to the least well-off students, who will also get £2700 from the Government by way of a £1500 grant and £1200 in fee remission if the family income is £15K or less, the £2700 phasing out by the time family income reaches £32K; the maximum Loan will increase to £4400 (more in London). The chairman of the Russell Group expressed the fear that all this is for the universities 'too little, too late' (Professor Sterling, *Times*, 8/1/04), since it will be bringing in by 2008 c£1.25 billion extra each year against a funding short-fall estimated by the UUK at c£10 billion pa and will take average annual funding per student to c£6500 (where the 'unit of resource' was in 1990 after the first decade of cuts in HE finances): see the HEPI Report on the financial implications of the proposals within the Higher Education Bill at *www.hepi.ac.uk/articles*; the financial benefits for the universities and the costs to the taxpayer arising from LibDem, Conservative party and rebel Labour MPs' alternative proposals are also assessed, all in the context of the APR 18-30 2010 target of 50% and its implied growth of some 200K undergraduate places. This £6500 is about $10K, which will be less than the level of funding in the lowest tier of US public HEIs: hardly leaving the UK's in a position 'to compete with the world's best' as the White Paper hoped...The Higher Education Bill achieved its second reading on 27/1/04 by 316 votes to 311, and thus the last nail has, potentially, been driven into the coffin of the UK's world-class universities, sealing in the under-resourced fate of the 'top' institutions: Oxford, for example, by 2009 will barely add 2.5% to its turnover as a result of this too-little-too-late reform. In contrast, the '*Irish Times*' (2/2/04) carried the news that the equivalent of HEFCE proposes to Government that the best HEIs should be privatised so as to allow the Ireland to compete by 2025 with the knowledge-driven US economy.

2

US HIGHER EDUCATION
SIZE AND SHAPE

Just as the UK's 'New Labour' Government in its 2003 consultation document sets out 'the need for reform' and has thereby triggered its Conservative Party opposition into promising to abolish tuition fees (hence protecting the 'affordability' of HE for 'Middle England', at the proposed expense of reducing access to HE for 'Poor England' since, supposedly, overall HE will be shrunk better to match the current level of taxpayer subsidy), so there has been debate in the USA over the cost/accountability and affordability/accessibility of HE since Congress in 1997 expressed the frustration of 'Middle America' with the ever-increasing 'cost of college' by establishing the National Commission on the Cost of Higher Education (which reported speedily in 1998, *Straight Talk About College Costs and Prices*). The latest 2003 surfacing of the 'affordability' debate is the House Committee on Education and the Workforce referring to a 'crisis' and to 'growing public anxiety and even outrage over college costs'; and the McKeon Bill (HR 3311) proposes to deny access to some kinds of Federal student financial aid programmes where an HEI raises fees by more than twice the rate of inflation for more than two years in succession (opponents point to a history of unworkable price-controls). In this respect US HE is, of course, similar to the UK independent/private schools where the story also is of year-on-year above-inflation increases in tuition fees, as likewise with private health care insurance both in the UK and USA, given that medicine and education as service industries lack the scope for the productivity gains found in manufacturing or retailing.

Indeed, there is also perhaps the beginnings of a debate along White Paper lines in other EU countries over the affordability for the State/taxpayer of a free, open-access, mass HE system (for example, Vossensteyn, H. (2002) 'Shared interests, shared costs: student contributions in Dutch higher education', in Journal of Higher Education Policy and Management 24 (2) 145-154). An observer of the HE scene across the OECD countries might even be tempted to predict a slow but steady convergence towards the US norm of requiring an increasingly significant student/family contribution towards the cost of delivering HE. Canada, for example, reduced the taxpayer input to HE by c20% during the 1990s, and increased student fees by some 35%. It has been a similar story in Australia, with the possibility of significantly higher fees from 2005. Much the same has happened in New Zealand. The privatisation of Japan's system of 'National' universities has already been cited, as has middle-class flight from Galbraithian 'public-squalor' HEIs to newly-created 'private-affluence' HEIs in some other countries. France is contemplating HE reforms that some critics see as the end of a national public service. (See Newsletter No. 33, Fall 2003, of the Boston College Centre for International Higher Education at www.bc.edu/cihe for articles on Australia, Japan and France.) Can UK HE buck this trend, or can it now select the best aspects of the funding of the US system (essentially, it is less regressive than the UK system in that the rich pay more), and leave behind its weaker components (lower Middle America is perhaps too quickly trapped by steeply declining student financial aid (SFA) scales, the system at that point being perhaps too progressive)? In fact, a January 2004 OECD Report welcomes the UK Government's 'commendable' £3K tuition fees as 'a role model' for other OECD countries hoping to compete with the USA 'in a modern knowledge-driven economy'. Hence the aim of this book in exploring and clarifying our understanding of the economics of US HE, focusing on the dimensions of costing/pricing/accountability, affordability and access.

J-G. Mora & L.E. Vila, 'The Economics of Higher Education' (in R. Begg, 2003, Kluwer, *The Dialogue between Higher Education and Research*), note that 'there are economic reasons that support the fairness of a greater private share in the financing of higher education... the increasing of the tuition fees is a key aspect in this mode [sic; 'move'?] towards a better balance between public and private financing...' Indeed, way back in 1986, D.B. Johnstone (*Sharing the Costs of Higher Education*, The College Board), in a thorough and valuable comparative study looking at student financial aid in the US, the UK, Germany, France and Sweden, argued that cheap, heavily taxpayer-subsidised HE for all does not make economic nor social-equity sense: 'The evidence is overwhelming, in centrally-planned as well as in market-oriented countries, that free tuition and generous maintenance grants are insufficient in themselves to achieve socio-economic, ethnic, or regional distributions within the student population that mirror those distributions in the general population...[and hence it may need] even higher grants (like 'study wages') to under-represented students, coupled with reduced subsidies to over-represented students, [in order to] achieve a more equal distribution of student places' (emphasis added).

Johnstone went on to make the interesting observation: 'While US students view higher education as a very expensive, yet very valuable and pleasurable, experience for which they and their parents should expect to pay, British students view the universities (somewhat less the polytechnics) more as their proper workplace, not unlike the factory for their less fortunate age peers, and thus view study as a service they are performing for society which incurs an expense (the costs of living, as well as any tuition or fees) for which they should be paid rather than one [a service] that should be paid [for] by them or their parents...' In relation to the UK, he was not optimistic, given the 'thunderous' political protests from Middle England when the Conservative Government in 1984 proposed to charge tuition fees of up to £4K pa (sic) to the wealthy, that politicians would ever have the courage to make 'any significant shift in the proportion of costs currently borne by students, parents, and taxpayers'. In fact, loans did replace grants during the 1990s, and then in 1997 the £1000 flat-rate, means-tested tuition fee was introduced, thereby beginning to reduce a level of taxpayer support for students that was 'the most generous in the Western world': hence, the 2003 White Paper's proposed £3K fee is merely the continuation of a very slow recognition that the taxpayer has other priorities and burdens in society than financing the major part of the cost of higher education for the better-off.

With reference to the US, Johnstone noted that here the student's share of the cost of HE was 'already the heaviest of any nation', while that borne by parents was 'also already high by most comparative measures', and hence any further attempt to reduce the taxpayer burden would be 'increasingly unpopular politically', especially since it would also signal a retrenchment in the strong national commitment to the value of HE. Again, however, the burden has shifted during the 1990s, and is still shifting, further to the student/family, and, arguably, perhaps rather disproportionately to the poorer student/family.

Thus, as Johnstone concludes: '...each national system is trying: to assure equality of opportunity; to provide necessary funding for the universities; to become no more, and perhaps even a bit less, of a burden to the taxpayer; and to avoid undue political antagonisms on the part of either parents or students'. Since 1986, of course, the UK has doubled the size of its HE sector and (albeit nowhere near proportionately) increased HE as 'a burden to the taxpayer', and so now, in terms of finding the 'necessary funding for the universities', it is into this whirlpool of 'political antagonism' that the Blair New Labour Government, via the 2003 White Paper, has, rather bravely, launched itself... It remains to be seen whether it will be any more successful in reducing free(ish) HE as a middle-class

Welfare State perk than was Sir Keith Joseph as Secretary of State for Education in the mid-1980s Thatcher Conservative Government (when 'The Iron Lady' executed one of the very few U-turns of her political career once confronted by the parents of Middle England students and the 'thunderous' protest of vested interest!).

Key Source Material

In what follows much reliance has been placed on certain key sources, listed below and hereafter cited by author(s) only:

- Breneman, D.W., et al (1996) *ASHE Reader on Finance in Higher Education*. Washington: ASHE.
- Duderstadt, J.J. & Womack, F.W. (2003) *The Future of the Public University in America: Beyond the Crossroads*. Baltimore: Johns Hopkins University Press.
- Ehrenberg, R.G. (2000) *Tuition Rising: Why College Costs So Much*. Cambridge, Mass.: Harvard University Press. (See also R.K. Vedder, *Going Broke by Degree: Why College Costs Too Much*, 2004 forthcoming, The AEI Press.) (See also R.L. Geiger, *Knowledge and Money: Universities and the Paradox of the Marketplace*, 2004 forthcoming, Stanford University Press; D.L. Kirp, *Shakespeare, Einstein and the Bottom Line: The Marketing of Higher Education*, 2004, Harvard University Press; and D. Fossum et al, *Who's Counting? Federal Research and Development Funds at Universities and Colleges*, 2003, RAND.)
- Geiger, R.L. (2000) 'Politics, Markets, and University Costs: Financing Universities in the Current Era', Research and Occasional Paper Series, Center for Studies in Higher Education, University of California, Berkeley ('downloadable' from ishi.lib.Berkeley.edu/cshe).
- Kane, T.J. (1999) *The Price of Admission: Rethinking How Americans Pay for College*. Washington: Brookings Institution Press.
- McPherson, M.S. & Schapiro, M.O. (1998) *The Student Aid Game: Meeting Need and Rewarding Talent in American Higher Education*. *Princeton*: Princeton University Press.
- Middaugh, M.F. (2000) *Analyzing Costs in Higher Education: What Institutional Researchers Need to Know*. San Francisco: Jossey-Bass.
- NACUBO (2002) *Explaining College Costs: NACUBO's Methodology for Identifying the Costs of Delivering Undergraduate Education*. Washington: National Association of College and University Business Officers. (Report of the NACUBO Cost of College Project chaired by Richard Spies, and 'down-loadable' from the NACUBO

web-site at www.nacubo.org.)
- Paulson, M.B. & Smart, J.C. (2001) *The Finance of Higher Education: Theory, Research, Policy & Practice.* New York: Agathon Press.
- 'Paying for College' (2003), US News & World Report 'All-New Guide'. (See also the US News web-site for a wealth of data/rankings – viewed by 'US HE Inc.' with great suspicion, unless, of course, the HEI concerned happens to come top of a particular table! – at www.usnews.com/usnews/edu/college/rankings/rankindex-brief.php.)

Indicative of the continuing wide interest in 'the cost of college' issue are the following recent media examples of hefty tuition fee increases (Karen W. Arenson, *New York Times*, 18/1/03), 'the HE industry' feeling obliged to defend its value-for-money (National Association of Independent Colleges and Universities, Press Release, 19/5/03), and the sustained pressure to increase fees as State subsidy of HE steadily reduces (Alan B. Krueger, New York Times, 1/5/03)...

- *SUNY Trustees Vote to Raise In-State Tuition*, by 41% to $4800 for 2003/04: 'With the proposal, SUNY joins a flood of public universities across the nation that have been scrambling to cover rising costs, declining state aid and drops in endowment income and other revenues by rising tuition.' Berkeley, for example, is going for 25% or so.
- *Increase in Private College Tuition Remains Steady for 2003-04* (at 5.8%): 'Private college and university presidents understand the challenges students and their families face when it comes to financing higher education...They are working hard to minimize the impact of tuition increases, while maintaining the quality of education and training they provide...Student concerns about affordability remain quite real, as do our institutions' efforts to find new ways to enhance efficiency and reduce costs...To keep their costs as low as possible without sacrificing the quality that has made them the envy of the world, private institutions are relying on innovative business management practices, flexible administration, enhanced cost control, and improved efficiency. These factors, along with significant investments in institutional grant aid, have kept a personal and high-quality private college education affordable to students from all backgrounds'. (Or so asserts the HE lobby-group, while a May 2002 Report by John Immerwahr on 'The Affordability of Higher Education' for the National Centre for Public Policy and Higher Education (www.highereducation.org) shows that the great

American public has yet to be convinced: 83% agree that 'colleges need to do a better job of holding down the costs of higher education'! See also the Centre's 'Losing Ground' related report, 'Our conclusion regarding the affordability of a college or university education is this: Americans are losing ground'.)

- *Tuition Minefield at State Schools*: '...With projected budget deficits totalling $100 billion in coming months, many state legislatures have slashed funds to higher education...the share of public colleges' revenues from state subsidises has declined over the last two decades...State colleges, which typically charge much less than private colleges, have moved to increase tuition and [residential] fees...Last year, tuition at public four-year colleges jumped 9.6%...Pressures will continue for flagship state universities to price tuition like elite private colleges, which tend to charge high, market-driven tuition but provide grants and loans to low-income students. The students who would pay more under a high-tuition/high-aid policy are from well-off families. In return, they would get a higher-quality education with more diverse classmates. And, most important, public subsidies would be better aimed at those for whom they would make the most difference...Unless legislators have the courage to allow closer-to-market-level tuition combined with generous scholarships and loans for those in need, the quality of higher education at flagship state universities is bound to suffer.'

High Tuition Fees, High Student Financial Aid

The US HE 'system' is extensive (some 4000 HEIs, split about equally public and private, are catering for 15m students and spending $225b of GDP sourced roughly half and half from the taxpayer and from students/their families), and also diverse (some 65% of high school graduates proceed at 18 directly to HE, compared to 50% in 1975; arguably, US HE contains most of the world's best HEIs and also some of the worst; and only some 450 HEIs are 'research-active', the vast majority being 'teaching-only'); indeed, there are as many systems as States. More than twice the OECD average is spent on HE, with half of the money coming directly from students/families – an unusually high amount by OECD norms. (In the UK, however, the HE spend is just below the OECD average, involving mainly public rather than private money and with a disproportionate amount of the taxpayer input diverted for student financial aid rather than as direct spending in the lecture room.)

Of the 7.5m US full-time undergraduates 25% are in private HEIs, where 'the sticker-price' for tuition is c$18300 pa on average (within a range peaking at c$27500 (£18K) pa for Harvard, Yale, Princeton, MIT, Dartmouth, Cornell...) compared with c$4100 at the public HEIs (within a range reaching $7.5/8K (£5K) pa, while 'out-of-state' students pay between two and three times as much as those attending the HE system of the State in which they are resident, and where all fees are climbing rapidly – 20% this year in, for example, Ohio, Iowa, and North Carolina). Room & Board adds another $7-9K (£5/6K) pa, and, of course, the US 'Liberal Arts' u/g degree course lasts 4 years compared with the norm of 3 in the English HE system. Clearly, HE theoretically (depending on eligibility for grants) costs the student rather more at the average public US HEI than at an English HEI (say, $15-20K (£10-13K) for tuition over 4 years compared with only c$5K (c£3300) over 3 years, and assuming accommodation costs and 'opportunity costs' of being a f/t student rather than in f/t employment are broadly the same in the US and UK), and dramatically much more at a private HEI (say, $75-110K for fees!).

The White Paper proposed £3K pa fee from 2006 would take the current, three-year £3300 figure paid in full anyway by only some 40% of UK students to £9K (c$14K compared with, by then, (?) c$20/25K at the US public HEIs, and perhaps $30K-plus at the research-oriented flagship campus within each State HE system...): the White Paper is indeed aiming at a moving target in trying to keep the upper end of UK HEIs competitive in income terms with even the best of the US publics, let alone the top private HEIs! A maximum fee for new students only in 2006/07 of £3K (and hence not being charged to all students until 2009/10, and in the meanwhile increasing at RPI as against HE salary inflation at 1-1.5% higher, and with the Government at one point hinting that HEIs should use a third (sic!) of the extra income to fund bursary schemes) is clearly going to do nothing to close that UK-US 'moving target' gap in any realistic way (hence the Select Committee siding with the Russell Group of the elite UK HEIs in calling for £5K from 2006).

Yet, amongst those 'top' US HEIs and despite tuition fees currently at c$25-29K pa, 20 or so claim that they can meet all of the financial need of all their students as identified, initially, by the standardised means-testing of the Free Application for Federal Student Aid form which assesses student/parental income, reserves the right to check data against tax forms (and threatens a fine for lying), and will then share the resulting 'Student Aid Report' with up to six HEIs nominated by the student who hopes that thereby one or more will offer its own financial aid package beyond any Federal Pell grants/Stafford & Perkins loans (see www.fafsa.ed.gov). Most HEIs next apply their own criteria, probably using the College Board Web-based complex and comprehensive College Scholarship Service Profile (see www.profileonline.collegeboard.com/index.jsp) or the new '568 Group' top colleges shared financial aid methodology*, to reach an 'expected family contribution' (perhaps assessing income for both parents and any step-parents, and usually taking into account some of the equity in the family home). They might offer a high SAT-scoring (or occasionally even the stellar basketball player!) 'desirable' applicant a full financial aid package of grant/cheap loan/guaranteed campus job to close the gap. Most applicants, however, will be left with an annual gap ('unmet need') of around $6K at the average private HEI (but still costing 'only' c$9K (c£6K) for a middle-'Middle America' $65K (£42K) family even at expensive Princeton, at a 'sticker-price' of c$39K pa including accommodation); compared with a c$4K average gap at the publics. Note that the UK £42K family would be means-tested to pay full fees at £1125 this year - £3K in 2006? – and to lose c£1K of the £4K maximum (inadequate level of) loan, an 'expected family contribution' of c$3250.

In terms of access rather than affordability, however, the successful 'Poor America' applicant to a rich, top HEI will likely get a full and very 'user-friendly' SFA package based on grants, compared with the inadequate level of the loan-oriented UK 'deal' at any and all UK HEIs - even if tuition fees are paid by the State. (Moreover, the UK Government seems to think that, within the semi-deregulated fee cap of £3K pa, there will be scope to offer bursaries/book-grants/etc to some of the HEI's poorer students: this seems naïve in the context of the economics of US HE, and not least allowing for the cost of accurate and fair means-testing incurred by the US HEIs who also are able to recover a chunk of such expenditure through charges levied for the honour of even applying to the HEI let alone for it undertaking the SFA assessment. NB: an applicant could run up $500+ in these fees, over and above the fees for SATs results needed for college/university entry!) But back to the SFA packages found within US HE...Sometimes the student/parent (or even 'a financial aid consultant' acting on their behalf – naturally, for a fee!) will negotiate a 're-evaluated' (better!) package on the basis of additional information not elicited in the FAFSA process; otherwise, the gap will have to be closed by economies/sacrifices in the family budget or by student/parental borrowing at commercial rates of interest. The 'cheap loan' referred to above is often financed by corporate bonds raised by a consortium of HEIs trading on their good credit rating and, crucially, their ability to set their own tuition fees as the major source of institutional income (along with endowment yield in some cases).

Appendix 1, 'Chuck goes to College', describes in detail the application process for the 'Middle America' high school graduate.

*Such sharing within the 28 members of the '568 Group' is an attempt to dampen the wasteful free-for-all bidding war for good students: 'wasteful' because it led to rich families paying for SAT-coaching and then their offspring being given scholarship money needed by genuinely clever and poor students; '568' because of the exemption section in tough Federal competition law which arose from the 1991 semi-successful anti-trust prosecution of the 'Overlap Group' of top HEIs.

Table 1 (data extracted from *Paying for College*, 2003) shows the financial aid process at work in some of those 20 top US HEIs, and in selected publics: it is of relevance for the more detailed discussion of costing – pricing - accountability, affordability, and accessibility which follows chapter-by-chapter. Suffice for now to note that high fees are accompanied by high levels of student financial aid (SFA), thereby bringing down the average annual cost of attending a prestigious private HEI from c$35K (including accommodation) to $15-18K (£10-15K) after grants and also bringing it probably to less than the cost of attending a top public HEI as an 'out-of-state' student (where SFA is likely not to be as readily available) or indeed close to that of attending one of the more prestigious public HEIs as an 'in-state' student: in Table 1 Michigan (Ann Arbor),for example, tips in at c$14K pa and Berkeley at c$15K; cf a humble public HEI such as Kansas State University at c$8K. But there is also a trend towards the semi-privatisation of the State flagship campus institutions (now being called 'the public Ivies'!): the University of Georgia at Athens, for example, proposed to the State's Board of Regents that, from 2003/04, it should levy a 'research institution differential fee' of $1000 pa, partly to substitute for reduced State funding and partly because UGA-A is just too cheap at $1000 below the tuition at the average public, doctoral-granting university at c$4K pa.

So, how can Cornell, MIT, Stanford, et al, afford to make themselves affordable for, say, lower-middle 'Middle America' by discounting so substantially 'the sticker price'? And, when offering SFA in this way, do they also keep themselves accessible to 'Poor America'? Or does 'Poor America' live at home and attend the local community college for two years earning an 'Associate Degree'? Moreover, at what point does a public HEI, created with State funds to serve the locals of that particular US State, effectively become at least a semi-private institution as it recruits ever-more 'out-of-state' students paying higher 'economic cost' tuition fees? (The analogy, of course, is with some UK HEIs, notably LSE, which fill up with a third or more overseas students paying realistic, non-

UK/EU fees and hence try to escape becoming increasingly dependent on the declining value of the Queen's Shilling: and hope also to avoid the paradox of Government demanding of UK HEIs greater accountability and seeking to call the tune through increased micro-management, while at the same paying rather less to the HE Piper? This semi-privatisation 'on-the-quiet', in effect 'the LSE model', is being given serious consideration within Oxford (and elsewhere), with the emphasis on expanding 'taught masters' degree courses and recruiting to them mainly high fee overseas students.)

Table 1: Fees and Student Financial Aid at selected 'top' private and certain public US HEI's (from "Paying for College, 2003": see also www.usnews.com)

HEI	Tuition Fee or 'Sticker Price'	Room & Board	Total Cost	Av cost after grants given for need	Av Discount	% on need grants	Av loan for need	Av SFA package	% whose need fully met
Columbia	28,206	8,546	36,752	16,590	55	40	4,605	23,266	100
Cornell	27,394	8,928	36,322	18,994	48	41	6,453	24,214	100
Dartmouth	27,771	8,217	35,988	17,650	52	43	5,767	26,168	100
Duke	27,844	7,921	35,765	18,818	49	34	4,530	22,687	100
Harvard	27,448	8,502	35,950	15,468	58	46	1,809	23,713	100
MIT	28,230	7,830	36,060	17,856	52	51	4,165	22,983	100
Princeton	27,230	7,842	35,072	14,690	60	43	0	23,810	100
Notre Dame	25,852	6,510	32,362	17,116	48	38	5,028	22,031	100
Stanford	27,204	8,680	35,884	15,937	58	42	3,200	24,300	97
Vasser	27,950	7,340	35,300	18,220	49	51	4,011	22,502	100
Williams	26,556	7,227	33,786	14,929	57	38	2,938	23,181	100
Yale	27,130	8,240	35,370	18,487	50	37	5,159	25,195	100
Vermont	8,994	6,378	15,372			46		12,867	90
Pittsburgh	8,528	6,470	14,990			39		8,816	30
Michigan (AA)	7,806	6,372	14,178			29		10,969	90
Berkeley	4,200	10,608	14,808			42		11,441	59
Kansas City	3,444	4,500	7,944			27	3,352	5,640	26
Idaho State	3,136	4,410	7,546			29		7,066	97
Florida State	2,428	6,450	8,878			31	3,287	6,807	4

Reputation and Prestige

Brewer, D.J., et al (2002, *In Pursuit of Prestige: Strategy and Competition in US Higher Education*, New Brunswick: Transaction Publishers) provide an industrial/market economics analysis of US HE, noting that paradoxically 'it is envied around the world for its success' and yet also 'it is seriously stressed'. They see HEIs competing for students and other 'customers' either on the basis of reputation or prestige, sometimes both. The former means carefully and very consistently meeting customer demands/expectations and providing high levels of customer service/satisfaction/vfm (for example, you must supply me with a credible/marketable vocational degree that really will get me a job). The latter is more intangible, it defines 'the best' amongst universities and may well be an amalgam of ability to recruit clever students, possessing ivy-clad quadrangles and high-tech labs, boasting a famous football/basketball team, and gaining sizeable research income. Reputation can be built, and destroyed, fairly quickly, and especially in narrow/new market segments; prestige is brand image, taking time to build and eroding only (and hence perhaps deceptively) slowly, and is relative rather than absolute ('a rival good' within 'a zero-sum game'). The HEI can invest in enhancing one or the other; it may try to tackle both as its competitive strategy but could thereby overstretch itself financially.

When pursuing prestige it will be 'acutely aware of U.S. News and World Report rankings' and similar 'consumer guides' such as Baron's and Peterson's, as well as the Carnegie Classification, Nobel Prize-Winners, SAT-scores, etc. The pursuit of prestige is 'expensive and risky'. Prestige is 'costly to build and maintain', and especially in the research market and in relation to faculty salaries; some HEIs get it wrong with 'disastrous' financial consequences. The rewards of already having or successfully investing in and achieving prestige include (at least in the US) massive alumni and other private giving: people want to associate themselves with 'the best', with 'a real university'. Given the cost and time-scale, and uncertainty, involved in building prestige, it is not surprising that the new and rapidly growing US 'for-profit' HEIs (University of Phoenix, etc.) 'appear to shun prestige building'. For them, and many other public or 'not-for-profit' HEIs, there is a perfectly viable niche pursuing a reputation strategy, applying a strong customer focus to the benefit of students and at the same time probably commodifying (downgrading) the academic labour force ('high teaching loads, monitored output, less time for research', and certainly they have no truck with collegial/shared governance as a luxury for only the old and rich universities: see Tapper & Palfreyman, *Oxford and the Decline of the Collegiate*

Tradition, 2000, London: Woburn Press).

Arguably, since there are relatively few HEIs following 'the prestige research university' model of excellence, the real dynamic in US HE responsible for 'transforming the nature of higher education' are the reputation HEIs, even if the prestige HEIs grab all the media attention while catering for only a tiny share of those 15m students. The analogy is obviously with the White Paper's emphasis on concentrating research funding in only a few UK 'prestige' HEIs (Oxford, Cambridge, Imperial and UCL – now being talked of as the 'G5' within the Russell Group elite of 15/20) and persuading the rest that a future based on teaching/consultancy 'reputation' is not only a sustainable and but also perhaps an attractive future... Moreover, the true unsung heroes of US HE may be the humble community colleges in terms of their providing accessibility, and especially for part-time mature students (such part-time provision often being a Cinderalla aspect of a nation's HE system). Indeed, the recently-elected Governor Schwarzenegger of California, in proposing a State Budget for 2004/05 which cuts funding to the State's universities by 8-9 % (thereby forcing a fee increase of c10%), recognises the relative value-for-money of the State's community colleges network by awarding them a 4.4% increase. Interestingly, in the context of the UK capped-fees regime and of the McKeon Bill, 'The Terminator' also calls for 'a predictable, capped-fee policy' for tuition fee raises of no more than 10% pa and linked to the rate of growth of per-capita personal income in the State.

The January 2004 '2020 Vision' consultation document concerning the University of Oxford's strategic options very clearly (and appropriately) offers (only) a prestige route over the next fifteen years, by the end of which the University would be 25% bigger (at 20,000 students) and (become or remain?): 'A university of the highest rank globally...with exceptional scholarly resources...[and] A well-founded reputation as one of the top ten universities in the world and one of the top two in Europe...' One may query the sense in such expansion and the resultant dilution of endowment income per student, especially in the context of existing global competitors generally being rather smaller than Oxford currently is: see Palfreyman in the *Oxford Magazine*, No. 224, Eighth Week, Trinity Term 2004; also *Times Higher* (12/3/04) and *Independent* (11/3/04)..

3

COSTING, PRICING & ACCOUNTABILITY

What does it cost to deliver the US Liberal Arts undergraduate degree? The key fact is that, even at c$27.5K pa for tuition at the top private HEIs, the price does not cover the cost. The National Association of College and University Business Officers (NACUBO) 2002 Project Report, *Explaining College Costs*, is a response by the HE sector to the challenge set by Congress for more data to be supplied annually to students and their families on university/college costs, prices and subsidies; it notes:

- 'Cost exceeds price…by anywhere from a few hundred dollars to as much as $20,000 or more' (p 10); 'all students, even those who pay full tuition, are subsidized' (p 33); that subsidy on top of 'the sticker-price' is between $4K and $11K at the public HEIs, and between $1K and $20K at the private HEIs (p 33). (The $4-11K State subsidy is analogous in the UK to the HEFCE 'T' block-grant, as reinforced to varying degrees by the 'R' allocation dispersed competitively amongst HEIs on the basis of their RAE score: the so-called dual-support funding of teaching at all HEIs by a fairly standardised amount and the financing of research by very variable amounts.)
- 'the main drivers of cost at most colleges and universities are the direct educational expense of the faculty and the academic services that support instruction and student services' (p 10).
- 'the public substantially overestimates the price of college, usually by thousands of dollars' (p 12) [presumably because of the media publicity given to 'sticker-price shocks'].
- This NACUBO costing methodology excludes 'all expenses related to separate graduate and professional schools, research institutes, continuing education programs, and other important activities that involve few, if any undergraduate students' (pp 18/19).
- But it includes the general research expenditure at teaching/research HEIs, partly because of the problem of accurately distinguishing between 'joint products' (p 24) and also on the basis that the undergraduate benefits from being taught in a

research-active environment ('Departmental research is vital and has a direct impact on the value and quality of instruction provided to students. Any arbitrary attempt to distinguish between departmental research and instruction ignores the fact that the integration of research and education is a major strength of the nation's colleges and universities and directly benefits undergraduates. Including departmental research costs within the instruction category is beneficial and appropriate for all institutions...[and anyway, realistically] No simple and uniform method for disaggregating such research is available' (pp 27 & 28): note, however, in the UK the DfEE/HEFCE fixation with trying separately to account at HEI level for the use of 'T' and 'R' block-grant allocations; in both the UK and USA 'T' probably subsidises 'R', and especially where the publicly funded research-oriented HEI steadily becomes increasingly dependent on the flow of overseas (and in the US, out-of-state) students paying high tuition fees.

- Nor does the methodology (yet) address the vexed issue of factoring in 'the replacement costs of facilities' (p 24), i.e. capital elements that will make the total annual cost even higher ('the contribution of capital expenditures to the cost of an undergraduate education tends to be dramatically understated', p 30 – perhaps by as much as 25/40% according to Winston, in Middaugh, who also notes that even wealthy Harvard in calculating depreciation for the first time in the early-1990s converted an operating surplus of $34m into a deficit of $43m, a loss which, apparently, could have been c$400m if the opportunity cost of capital had also been taken into account!).

- The methodology incorporates 'the net cost of auxiliary enterprises' (campus bookstores, student housing and catering, and intercollegiate athletics – noting that 'in only a few institutions do revenues from intercollegiate athletics exceed their costs'!, p 29).

- The cost of SFA 'may be viewed as either an investment in educational quality or a price discount to fill otherwise empty seats' (p 29) – Geiger, for example, asserts that 'Private university education, on average, is over-priced, so that it can be sold at a discount. Public university education is under-priced [mainly because of] political constraints'! Indeed, discounting as a form of 'price-war' has increased from 27% of the theoretical collectable total in 1990 to 40% by 2002: discounting has become the norm; it is another enrolment/marketing device, with 80% of undergraduates getting a discount in 2000 compared with 63% in 1990.

In essence, therefore, Price = Cost – Subsidy (where Subsidy is the non-tuition revenue as a catch-all category for any revenues from non-student sources), and hence 'it can be seen that rising tuition rates could be due to either rising costs [as especially in the private HEIs], or falling subsidies [as broadly so in the ordinary public HEIs], or a combination of the two forces [as probably in the research-active flagship State HEIs attempting to keep pace with the leading private HEIs]...' (Paulsen & Smart, 15). The economics of US HE and of US HEIs is a topic much studied, dating back to pioneering work by Bowen (*The Costs of Higher Education*, 1980) who identified HEIs as driven to maximise costs in line with any expectation of rising revenue from tuition fees, endowment yield, alumni donations, State grants, corporate bond borrowing, and the like. They are, after all, 'not-for-profit' (charitable) organisations that have no need at all to generate a surplus to reward share-holders; they exist to deploy all revenue to achieve maximum 'outputs' of teaching and research.

Revenue Maximisers and Cost Minimisers

In Breneman et al, Bowen discusses the 'laws' of US HE: HEIs seek 'educational excellence, prestige, and influence'; each HEI 'raises all the money it can' and promptly 'spends all it can' (HEIs as 'revenue maximizers' and 'cost minimizers'); 'The question of what ought higher education to cost...does not enter the process except as it is imposed from the outside...[by] legislators, students and their families'. Ehrenberg, in pre-empting the NACUBO study and noting that students at the top private HEIs 'get a lot more than they pay for' (p 11), also explores why the private HEIs seem unable to hold down costs: fancy infrastructure provision, science research, collegial governance avoiding awkward and painful cost control issues, salaries for academic super-stars, SFA, student recruitment efforts, subject segmentation/proliferation, inefficient utilisation of space, IT and library costs, and sports teams that lose money... but 'As long as lengthy lines of highly qualified applicants keep knocking at its door and accepting its offers of admission, no institution has a strong incentive to unilaterally end the spending race' (p 14).

In terms of the accountability of these HEIs to 'Society', Ehrenberg argues that 'to maintain broad public support these institutions will have to continually demonstrate that they remain accessible to students from all socio-economic backgrounds [pp 267 and 268]...selective private institutions that continue to raise their tuition by much more than the rate of inflation, that back off of their commitment to maintain accessibility, and that continue to exhibit large endowment growth, may well be courting potential disaster. They will be almost 'asking' to be regulated [p 269]...selective private higher education is not immune to changing public concerns and policies. It would be very prudent for these institutions to think more now about increasing the efficiency of their operations and holding down costs [p 284]': the 2004 McKeon Bill looms!

Again, there is an interesting US/UK analogy: here between US private HEIs and UK private schools, given that each has been able in recent years to ratchet up fees which a compliant set of customers continue to pay, seemingly with minimal protest, the extra income not (admittedly) being used for distribution as excessive profits to shareholders but to fund ever-grander (and perhaps not always vital) infrastructure and, in the case of the US HEIs, the inflating salaries of 'trophy professors' (and, indeed, both groups have also been investigated over alleged 'fee-fixing' by the competition authorities under anti-trust/cartel legislation; in addition, there are occasional questions raised about just how effective is their deployment of charitable income: see Palfreyman, chapter 7 of Walford, G. (editor) *British Private Schools* (London: Woburn Press, 2003) for an analysis of the politics of charitable status).

Market Forces

An issue of Higher Education Quarterly (Vol. 57, No. 2, April 2003) is devoted to 'the increasing visibility of market mechanisms' in national systems of HE, which 'will have a major impact on higher education policy in forthcoming years' (Editorial). Jongbloed's article (focussing on the Netherlands) explores 'marketisation policies', albeit that 'in reality a true market for higher education does not exist in many countries' because only rarely can 'the basic conditions' for a free market be fulfilled; 'a cleverly designed balance of government regulation, price signals, monitoring instruments, quality assurance policies, and so on' is needed 'to correct for market failures or potential imbalances between private and social benefits'. Steier notes, across OECD countries, the growth of private expenditures relative to public expenditures (indeed, the c25% private HE in the USA is now almost matched in the Czech Republic, Hungary, Poland, and Romania, and is easily exceeded in the Philippines, Korea, India, Indonesia, and in most of Latin America). Dill suggests there is a downside to the US case of 'allowing the market to rule'; he provides 'an assessment of the relative social costs and benefits of market competition' which challenges the more positive analysis of Hoxby* in seeing market competition as having created an efficient system of baccalaureate/undergraduate education and in concluding that a truly free market is the most effective public policy. Dill queries 'whether these continually increasing college and university expenditures actually produce benefits for the larger society', whether 'the potential exists for market imperfections', and whether 'allowing the market to rule in higher education would be a particularly naïve choice for policy makers'. (* Hoxby's 2001/02 material is at http://post.economics.harvard.edu/faculty/hoxby.)

Massy, W.F. (2003) *Honoring the Trust: Quality and Cost Containment in Higher Education*, explores US HE, warts and all, seeking to balance quality and cost in delivering teaching and research. It is not comfortable reading for those in US HE; they must re-earn the public's trust ('colleges and universities are not all they can be... the gap represents a breach of trust that needs to be repaired'). To do that they need to develop a second core competency besides research; they need to concentrate more effort on teaching and learning, on quality control and cost control, on the student side of the HEI in an age of massification, consumerism and marketisation: something already being done elsewhere, outside the US. How then has US HE got away with increasing tuition fees remorselessly? - 'Higher education can indulge itself because the market power enjoyed by its highly selective and name-brand segments provides a pricing umbrella for other institutions... Market power confers self-reinforcing advantages, and the circle is not necessarily virtuous... price-quality associations reinforce the circularity and the positional arms race...' In short, US HE is a 'very inefficient' marketplace: an inefficiency matched only by its 'fuzzy understanding of its teaching and learning processes' and its inability to accurately cost its activities within a culture of rampant cross-subsidy (even if such cross-subsidy is 'a good thing' in that it is 'the legitimate exercise of academic judgement').

That said, the teaching-to-research cross-subsidy may mean that students paying high tuition fees do not get value for money, unless one accepts a key concept and premise: that a teacher who is an active researcher is a better teacher, and the undergraduate benefits accordingly; and also that it is anyway virtually impossible accurately to split academic time between research and tuition (but Massy argues that HEIs could at least try an estimate, citing UK HE's 'diary studies' of academic use of time). He concludes that, at least in high tuition private research HEIs, the undergraduate helps pay for research, and hence, in tuition terms, may not get what he/she is paying for; but he/she does get a hefty private rate of return from a college degree awarded at a prestigious (research active?) HEI (especially if followed up by a graduate school at a similar HEI), and hence gets overall value for money. Which is not to say that a marginal shift in emphasis from research to tuition would not be inappropriate in the name of economic efficiency and re-earning public trust: '...research does boost educational quality, but it's possible to have too much of a good thing... the balance between research and education has tilted too far towards research as the so-called academic ratchet pushes an institution inexorably [towards 'research intensity' at the expense of 'quality of education']...' And, in the absence of quality control, nobody notices the steady clicking of the ratchet and the resultant 'quality degradation' in teaching and learning: the academic ratchet at best 'inhibits the improvement of core educational competency', and at worst becomes 'a corrosive force'. What is needed is greater academic audit and better motivators of improved educational competency, and a deeper understanding of just what is quality in teaching and learning to go alongside greater cost consciousness, analysis and control: all needed to rebuild the core competency in education and regain public trust.

On attempts at and problems implementing cost control within US HE see also W.A. Brown & C. Gamber, *Cost Containment in Higher Education*, 2002, Jossey Bass: Ashe-Eric Report (18,5). The key issue is academic productivity, and (for the HEI manager) that amounts to trading off reduced research time against greater teaching time (and teaching in larger class sizes): anathema, of course, to most academics seeking the career kudos that research brings. Academic tenure itself, however, is not necessarily 'a bad thing', in that the downside of inflexibility for the HEI (seen as job security by the individual academic) probably means getting away with (as the upside for the HEI) paying salary levels uncompetitive with the private sector: that said, the increased use of part-time, untenured faculty is a clear route to cost saving (the casualisation of the academic labour force). There is little scope to save on premises, given maintenance backlogs; outsourcing facilities management and improved energy management may, however, offer useful savings. The HEI will probably need to ask very awkward questions about the real value (and true cost) of its research activities; can it afford them and their related overheads (the US 'for profit', commercial HEIs, of course, shun such 'loss-leader' research)? Finally, and paradoxically, State attempts at increased monitoring of, and demands for, greater accountability from HEIs may well hamper their attempts at cost containment, or even increase compliance costs and hence overall costs.

Thus, the UK may not wish to let HE become completely 'marketised', given the concerns of some observers of US HE over market inefficiencies, lack of cost and quality controls, and research trumping undergraduate teaching ('the academic ratchet'); equally, however, the prospect of UK HE sliding towards the EU under-resourced, over-crowded public sector norm is hardly enticing, and the status quo is clearly unsustainable as public funding fails to keep pace with student numbers.

See Appendix 2, 'Pricing the Product: Manic-Marketplace or Cosy Cartel?', for a discussion of the costing and pricing issues potentially to be faced by UK HEIs if the proposed minimal degree of semi-deregulation of tuition fees occurs in 2006.

An Arms-Race

Such an arms-race amongst the top private US HEIs is fuelled partly by charging increasingly high tuition fees, partly by income from endowment, partly by alumni-giving, and partly by using bond financing as an extra funding stream (still unknown, or at least unexplored, in the UK). Yet, as Ehrenberg shows (pp 36 & 45), there are big differences across the elite range of HEIs: for 1997 Princeton's annual endowment income per student was $31K, Harvard's $24.5K, Stanford's $14K, Cornell's $4.5K, and Duke's $4K (Oxford's is c£3500/$5250); annual alumni-giving at Princeton per alumnus was $1075 (worth $21K per current student), at Harvard $844 ($23K), at Stanford $987 ($21K), at Cornell $675 ($11K), and at Duke $379 ($18.5K). All of this is reflected in faculty salaries, where a full/tenured professor in 1997/98 was on $117K (c£75K) at Harvard, $111K at Stanford, $110K at Princeton, $101K at Duke, and $90K at Cornell. At Oxford the upper end of the salary scale was then about $60K (c£40K); a feeble amount easily beaten at the private, but also at the better US public HEIs: Berkeley $93K, Michigan $92K, North Carolina $86K, Penn State $83K, Wisconsin $74K. The picture for junior academics is similarly depressing for the Brits: Oxford at c$40K, MIT $61K, Stanford $60K, Duke $54K, Berkeley $52K, Wisconsin $50.5K...(Ehrenberg, pp 116/117).

Clearly, the major factor in keeping UK HE 'cheap', if not especially 'cheerful', as it has 'massified' over the past 15 years is academic salaries being held at low levels by this comparison with the USA and also in relation to comparable UK groups (where a gap of c30% has opened up: although, probably, US academics also argue that their salaries have not kept pace with comparable professional groups). For Oxford this has meant, as its 2003 'HR Strategy' document notes, 'serious recruitment and retention problems', with the average number of applicants per post advertised falling 'by one-third over the last four years' as potential applicants are put off by 'the very high cost of living in Oxford, where house prices approach those in London'. Moreover, anecdotal evidence suggests that Oxford may find not a few of its first-choice candidates for academic jobs take one look at the house prices in the estate agents' windows and conclude that they are not able to afford to accept the Oxford offer: how long does it need before a world-class university winds down towards mediocrity as second-choice and even third-choice people are appointed and in turn appoint in their own image?

That said, if the US Ivy League HEIs ever could end the salary arms-race in competing for 'trophy professors' on $150K pa, and even up to $300K (and assuming that their academic super-stars were not then poached by European HEIs newly entering the arms-race), it is unlikely that the quantum of scholarship and research provided to academe would be seriously reduced because the academics concerned were moon-lighting doing low-grade consultancy to make ends meet. Whether there is or is not a potentially wasteful arms-race amongst top US HEIs, Geiger (in D. C. Levy, 1986, *Private Education*, OUP) sees the existence of a sizeable private sector within US HE as entirely positive, not least in HE thereby avoiding a dangerous over-dependence, as in the UK, on the politically fickle financial largesse of Government, with also all the attendant risk (now, sadly, in the UK an alarming reality) of stultifying bureaucratic and centrist micro-management by Government: '...the continual search for private resources shapes the existence of private colleges and universities. The unique relationship that each independently acting institution develops with student clienteles and donor constituencies ultimately determines its distinctive character. The perpetual quest for resources, then, is the true wellspring of diversity in American higher education...[Such diversity] enhances the adaptability of the [HE] system as a whole, and ipso facto the responsiveness of the system to society's needs...'

US Public HEIs

Turning to the US public HEIs, the main driver of tuition fee increases has been the steady retreat of the taxpayer in terms of how much the States will pay; in the UK, of course, the taxpayer has also retreated over the past 20 years, but the HEIs have not been given the political freedom (even if, technically, they possess the legal autonomy) to (partially) compensate by levying tuition fees (or not, at least, until the flat-rate, 'min-max' £1000 fee was introduced some 4 years ago). In the USA the Federal Government has also retrenched in its level of funding for HE, mainly by failing to keep the value of the Pell Grant (running at c$11b pa across c4.5m recipients), Stafford subsidised loans, and similar, matched to the climb in tuition fees. In fact, the Bush Administration announced an actual cut, as reported in *The New York Times* (13/6/03, Greg Winter,

'Change in Aid Formula Shifts More Costs to Student'). The effect, varying according to the levels of State taxes, of the changes in 'the small print' of the needs-analysis calculations will be a further move to reliance on loans and/or part-time work to pay for HE, as discussed in the 'Access' chapter below, with the $25K family now getting some c$150-225 pa less in Federal SFA (c$500-950 at $50K, and c$750-1500 at $80K) and with the Federal budget saving 'billions of dollars'. In other words the 1960's 'implicit partnership' of Federal Government and the States to make HE affordable and accessible 'has come unravelled' during the 1990s (Paulsen & Smart, pp 321/322), as HE has lost out in the prioritising of public expenditure.

That said, even at the same time as the taxpayer pays the piper less Government has also called more of the tune (albeit to nowhere near the extent in the UK), an accountability process which Mumper explores in Chapter 8 of Paulsen & Smart: in some States tuition fees have been capped, in some there is performance funding of HE, many have sought 'to mandate improved efficiency and productivity' (24 States in the mid-1990s 'began to question how faculty members spend their time', p 334). Geiger refers to 'a curious animus against universities and the academic world', to a 'prevailing mood of suspicion', in the 1990s when 'dubious policy initiatives can be related directly to the prevalence of negative cliches', where 'meddling was motivated by outright distrust', and all this intervention was done in the name of accountability. (Even so, HE in the US as a country with a federal political structure generally seems to have been protected from the worst excesses of the UK's quango-mad and acronym-ridden control-freak regime fostered by an over-centralised system of government where a daft idea can rapidly become policy and be implemented nation-wide. The 2004 Higher Education Bill is in parts yet another example.)

Moreover, most States have also questioned the efficiency and value of a low-tuition fee policy and have moved to a high-tuition/high-aid model; some have capped enrolment at the State's flagship/research and hence more costly HEIs, and encouraged growth at the lower cost HEIs (especially at the two year 'Associate Degree' community colleges); almost all have developed tax-advantageous prepayment and savings bond programmes for families to finance HE...But, given the pressure on the public purse from competing demands (policing, the military, schools, welfare, health, etc) the best that US public HE can hope for is to 'moderate the rate of declining affordability and to protect the most disadvantaged from its full effect' (p 348). Thus, Geiger sees 'privatization' as the 'overarching theme' of US HE during the 1980s and 1990s, witnessed by 'especially the transfer of the burden of support to students and their parents' from the taxpayer, and bringing with it a HE system which has 'served the aspirations of advantaged students over disadvantaged ones': and there is no hint that such educational opportunities 'will not continue to be reaped disproportionately by the more privileged sectors of American society'.

Duderstadt & Womack contemplate the future of the US public HEI:

- US public HE is increasingly unable to compete with other social priorities, and also it is being viewed politically more as 'an individual benefit rather than a societal right'. Thus, the US taxpayer steadily retreats from financing the public HEIs at the levels of a generation ago.

- Yet, even as the public HEIs compensate for this reduction in State funding by increasing tuition fees, the State universities still remain 'affordable' for 'Middle America', especially since politicians 'in an effort to buy votes' are subsidising clever middle-class kids at the expense of properly financing access for poor kids. A regressive funding policy that amounts to 'a profound misunderstanding of the fact that educational access and opportunity are achieved not through subsidising those who can afford to pay but, rather, by providing financial assistance to those who cannot' (a point, of course, at present lost on 'Old Labour' MPs, the TUC, the NUS, NATFHE and the AUT as they all lobbied against the White Paper's proposed £3K fee).

- And this subsidy may mean 'Middle America' gradually deciding that its children need not 'attend an expensive private institution, when they could attend their flagship state institution for less than 20 per cent of the cost'.

- Moreover, these elite public HEIs are effectively being deregulated and semi-privatised as they are given greater freedom to increase their tuition fees and to manage themselves.

- But they are now facing competition from 'aggressive and intrusive' private HEIs and their 'predatory recruiting' in 'irresponsible faculty raids' where their senior academic staff are poached. The authors warn of a possible political backlash if 'the public universities are compelled to fight back by unleashing the T word, 'tax policy', and question the wisdom of current tax policies [in the form of charitable relief] that sustain vast wealth and irresponsible behaviour at a cost to both taxpayers and to their public institutions'. (Hence, very recently, Harvard has announced a policy of waiving almost all its fees for even average income US families, let alone for 'Poor

America'.)

- There is also potentially serious competition for both public and 'not-for-profit' private US HE from the growing 'for-profit' private sector ('the tsunami of commercial online education') as HE shifts from being a cottage industry 'ripe for the unbundling of activities' into 'a period of fundamental restructuring of the enterprise itself' (indeed 'as in other deregulated industries' there may well be institutional casualties), and especially as public HE can no longer assume that the State 'will shield it from market competition'.
- Such commercial HE is all the more threatening since traditional US HE, still managed and governed in an 'amateurish' way, 'has yet to take the bold steps to contain cost increases which have been required in other sectors of society such as business and industry'; these new competitors will challenge the existing 'high-cost, low-productivity paradigm'.

The HEI as a Black Box

Geiger also explores the link between high-cost HE (supported by high tuition fees and in some cases large endowment) and high-quality HE, conceding that this is 'something of a black box'. The spend per student at the prestigious private HEIs is given as $35-50K pa (Princeton $51K, Harvard $46K, Yale $38K, etc), compared to some $25K at the average private university (Columbia, Cornell, Chicago, Northwestern) and c$20K at the top State HEIs (Berkeley, Michigan-AA, North Carolina-CH), and to $10-12K at the low end of the range of public universities (Florida State, Kansas, Louisiana): cf the UK Government's 'unit of resource' for 'T' at c£5K ($7500) pa. Following the NACUBO format referred to above, and comparing with the figures just quoted, Oxford spends annually (depending on the academic subject) c£18.5K ($28K) per undergraduate (the exact figure is calculated in an OxCHEPS study on the costing and pricing of Oxford, as detailed in Appendix 3; adding in capital depreciation could add a third to that amount as discussed above). Why the difference, and is Princeton exactly five times better at $50K than Florida State at $10K? 'Peering into the black box' he asserts that the costs, and quality, varies as follows in the economics of delivering US HE: mix of teaching programs (medicine, science, engineering and doctoral programs in anything are costly), staff/student ratios (about 50% better in the private HEIs), academic salaries (some 25% lower in the public HEIs), facilities/space (is the infrastructure of private Stanford across the Bay from public Berkeley noticeably more extensive and rather better maintained?), research ('highly rated departments are costly for universities to establish and sustain'), and 'talented student peers' (as recruited, at a cost, by merit-based SFA).

So, in the US most States are prepared to spend more annually per student, whether by way of direct taxpayer funding or by allowing their public HEIs to charge realistic tuition fees, than is the UK, although admittedly the US HEIs do have a major additional cost element in the form of providing a whole army of academic advisers/counsellors needed to steer confused students through the smorgasbord of the Liberal Arts degree courses and to assist with study skills/remedial writing. In Oxford's case (see Appendix 3) the essential problem is that, having (in retrospect unwisely) stretched the endowment base across far too many students as 'cost-drivers' by allowing under-funded growth, the University is left trying to sustain a tutorial teaching system which depends on an anachronistically generous (by UK HE norms) staff/student ratio and at the same time also has to support an excessive volume of 'Big Science' research activity on which it has negligently failed to recover an appropriate level of overhead*. In short, Oxford's financially unsustainable strategy increasingly unravels as Government reduces 'T' funding nationally but refuses to fully deregulate tuition fees, as the University itself fails to control its growth and the consequential dilution of endowment, and as its science departments become victims of their academic success in boosting (while boasting of) the level of (inadequately-costed and hence rather under-priced) research. Oxford is attempting to operate at the upper end of the US HE market in terms of both being a committed Liberal Arts teaching institution along the lines of, say, Dartmouth College and a broad-based research-focused Harvard, Stanford or Yale. It has the endowment for the former and a little of the latter, and by sacrificing teaching it could have the endowment for a fair chunk of the latter, but it has not got the resources to be a Dartmouth and a Harvard when it is too timid to charge the tuition fees of the former and is half a century behind building up the alumni-giving of the latter. And as for the wisdom of the 25% increase to 20,000 students floated in its '2020 Vision' 2004 consultation planning document...

Thus, the University's 'best-guess' of the aspiration annual 'deficit' is £20m on the teaching side, and £60m for research; some £80m in the context of a c£500m turn-over (again, see Appendix 3). The University's current (and strategically irrational?) response seems to be to devalue its 'USP', 'prime product' in the form of 'the Oxford Tutorial' (see Palfreyman, *The Oxford Tutorial*, 2001, 'down-loadable' from the OxCHEPS web-site at oxcheps.new.ox.ac.uk) and exit from a niche which it dominates, while attempting to compete exclusively and more aggressively in a niche where it has to face Harvard, Yale, Stanford, Cornell, Columbia, Chicago and Princeton as universities properly in control of their own destiny by following a large endowment/high tuition fee winning strategy. Moreover, as stressed in R.J. Light (2001) *Making the Most of College: Students Speak Their Minds* (Cambridge, Mass.: Harvard University Press), students value as the best learning experience those courses which are offered in 'highly structured' and 'small is better' classes/seminars which demand 'significant amounts of writing' (at least 60, and even over 100, A4 pages per academic year): 'including extensive writing in classes does much to enhance student engagement' (p 58). Such intensive teaching is a key recruitment factor for the US Liberal Arts colleges; indeed, in some respects these small (and very expensive) HEIs resemble the UK's small-class (and in some cases equally expensive) private schools: the 'Dead Poets Society' meets 'Mr Chips'!

* The average overhead/indirect cost recovery rate for US private universities is given as 64% against 43% for the public universities in Hoenack, S.A. & Collins, E.L. (1990) *The Economics of American Universities* (New York: State University of New York Press): Oxford currently manages just over 40%, and UK HEIs overall achieve barely 15% against actual overhead costs of between 50% and 150% depending on the academic area...Perhaps the simplest and single most effective step that Government could take to protect the global status of Oxford, Cambridge, Imperial and UCL, and one avoiding much of the political hassle relating to the all-too-timid step of increasing fees to only £3K, is to ensure that the UK research councils are sufficiently funded to pay adequate levels of overheads. At the same time the HEIs themselves must be more robust in not donating their resources to their research partners by under-costing 'R'. (See also the HEPI Report on the 'dual-funding' regime for financing research, at the 'Articles' Page of *www.hepi.ac.uk*.)

4

AFFORDABILITY

Baum, in Paulsen & Smart (Chapter 2), notes that 'many educators and policy analysts are critical of the shifting focus away from the accessibility of higher education for low-income students towards affordability for middle-income students', given that 'affordability is not an absolute concept' ('for most families the issue is what other goods and services they will have to sacrifice in order to pay for college'), and also given that anyway 'a college education is an investment, with the benefits enjoyed over a lifetime'. In addition, while undoubtably 'the cost of attending college has increased much more rapidly in recent years than either the prices of other goods and services or family incomes' (in real terms it has doubled at both public (up 120%) and private HEIs (up 110%), 1971/72-1999/00, while GDP and personal disposable income each grew by only about 50%) and while 'the sticker-price' is now frighteningly high at the private HEIs, it is discounted for most students and only 7% paid more than $20K in 1999. That said, the 'average', as ever, hides good and bad news: for high-income US families 'the cost of college' as a %age of their annual income has barely increased over the 30 years, but for 'Middle America' it has gone from c30% to c45% at a private HEI and from 13% to 17% at a public HEI, while for 'Poor America' the figures are 90% to 160% and 40% to 60%.

Thus, affordability is not an issue for 'Rich America': the private HEI may as well keep 'the sticker-price' moving in line with their family income, so long as it can afford to discount to some degree for the middle group and substantially for the lower group; in the case of the former to fill the lecture theatres, and in the case of the latter to have some claim to enhancing social mobility. In effect, the 1960s/1970s era of HE as 'cheap'/ 'a free(ish)-good' has ended in the US sooner than in Australia, rather sooner than is (likely to be?) the case in the UK, and probably much sooner than will be the (inevitable?) case in the European systems. US HE has indeed become less 'affordable' for 'Middle America', but it has not stopped buying the product (45% of 'Young America' went to college in 1960 before it got 'cheap', and 65% in 1998) no matter how much it moans about the price, and it is still accessible for 'Middle America' even if no longer such a bargain.

A complex, and perhaps crucial, aspect is the degree to which US HE can sustain these ever-increasing tuition fees, long since at higher levels than in the UK and Europe, partly because US middle-income families pay rather less by way of income tax and in other taxes (notably on petrol/gas), and hence not only do not necessarily expect HE to be a Welfare State free-good but also can anyway utilise their greater disposable income to help their kids pay their way through the four or even five years of college; similarly, 'Young Graduate America' presumably can cope with the monthly repayments on its larger student debt because it too carries less of a tax burden than its UK/European counterparts. And, perhaps above all, education is part of 'the American Dream'; Americans really believe in and properly value 'Going to College', and are (within reason) prepared to pay for such a self-improvement process.

So, just how far dare the UK Government push Middle England (whether as parents providing financial help to their student children, or as graduates in their twenties and thirties repaying student debt), already heavily taxed by US standards, into further (and not very) 'hidden taxation' by way of increased HE tuition fees? Will 'New Labour' really risk the ire of those benefiting from UK HE as an unofficial Welfare State perk for the better-off by eventually ending an unjust and wasteful blanket subsidy?

That said, it would seem unlikely, now that UK HE has 'massified' and hence such a high proportion of middle-class school leavers go on to HE, that there is any longer such a cultural difference (at least for the middle-class young) whereby 'Going to College' was perhaps once more valued and the aspirational norm in the USA than in the UK: the issue is whether the individual student (and his/her family) in the US has simply become more used to meeting a greater share of the cost while still seeing HE as necessary and worthwhile, whereas in the UK we have yet to make this belated adjustment from times when the State could afford generous financial support to a much smaller student population and also to fund HEIs twice as well. The 'affordability debate' in US HE, however, has another dimension: 'Colleges are using more of their financial aid funds to attract desirable [high SAT-scoring] students and to compete with other institutions [on 'merit-aid'] and are focusing less on increasing access for those who cannot afford to pay ['needs-blind' admission]...' In other words, the politicians, having terminated the 1960s/1970s concept of cheap-or-even-free public HE, end up seeking middle-class votes by utilising HOPE Scholarships and the like to make HE less costly for the middle-income (and more politically powerful?) families, while (as discussed in the next chapter on 'Access') not bothering to index the value of financial aid to students from poorer (and politically insignificant?) families.

Tuition Discounting

In Paulsen & Smart, Breneman et al (Chapter 12) explore 'the role of tuition discounting'. They see it: as 'a critical strategic tool in enrollment management', 'a necessary tool to recruit and retain students'; as a 'technique' used 'to mold a 'desirable' student profile' and to compete with not only other private HEIs but also with the flagship public institutions; as a practice also now being picked up by the better public HEIs; as being increasingly a matter of offering loans as SFA rather than grants; as shifting 'need-blind' towards 'merit-aid' tempered by at best 'need-aware'; as eating into the overall tuition fee 'take' in that, after the cost of SFA, net tuition was 75% of gross tuition in 1990 and only 63% by 1999; and as being the start of a price-war that may destabilise the finances of some private HEIs not possessing the padding of substantial endowment income. This last point is echoed by Ehrenberg and other observers of US private HE; McPherson & Schapiro compare tuition fee discounting in HE with the discounting of airline tickets! They are saddened by SFA becoming 'a competition weapon': 'When recruitment pressures make financial aid letters look like they are written by the same people who write the marketing brochure, we are all in trouble.'

Geiger stresses that US HE has remained within the financial reach of 'Middle America', even if less affordable than in the high public subsidy 1960s/1970s, because a new source of funds has been tapped in the form of loans: '...the future earnings of students (and in some cases parents) were transformed through loans into current expenditures [and thereby] permitted students to extend their outlays to keep pace with the rising level of tuition'. It is 'the rise of the student loan culture', together with tuition discounting, which has kept the lecture rooms full: 'Under these conditions, student resistance to price increases in an economic sense (i.e. reduced demand), especially at the more prestigious and expensive institutions, has been virtually nil' (Geiger, p 5). US HE is, therefore, a very price inelastic good. That said, whether in post-Enron and post-Dotcomboom America as parents rebuild diminished pension plans, and as the Federal Government reduces loan capacity, the high-tuition party will end with a monumental hangover for US HE remains to be seen... (And indeed much the same question must surely hang over the continued ability of UK independent schools to get away with well-above-inflation hikes in fees – 10% for 2003/04 at 4x RPI.)

Arguably, the US HE boom of the last twenty years has been fuelled, like so many other aspects of 'The American Way of Life', by massive borrowing as the US economy has sucked in global investment and expanded the national debt, an economic bubble so far only partially deflated by the stock market collapse of the past three years and by the very recent beginning of the decline of the $ against other currencies: see Richard Duncan, 2003, *The Dollar Crisis: Causes, Consequences, Cures* (Singapore: Wiley). If the Duncan thesis is correct, US HE is indeed in for a difficult time as the States retreat even further from funding public HE (ultimately a mere discretionary budget item compared with health care, schools, and policing) and as the annual total return on the endowments of the private HEIs revert to the rather lower mean than the double-digit growth enjoyed in the 1990s. Moreover, perhaps neither public nor especially private HEIs will any longer be able to take for granted that the sticker-price can each year be hiked since an already financially stretched 'Middle America' may become consumer-resistant to yet more family debt in order to fund Junior going to college at any price. A crisis in the US economy, however, will surely impact also on the UK, as another of the few net importer nations, leaving UK HE facing another decade or two of continuing financial retrenchment and of increasing polarisation between what could be the growing number of cheap(ish) teaching-only HEIs and far fewer expensive research-oriented, arms-race HEIs: at least, compared with US HE, UK HEIs generally are already used to being relatively 'lean and mean'.

The 'For-Profits'

Another interesting issue will be the degree to which, in the context of the WTO/GATS proposals for the freeing-up of trade in such services as HE and given potentially such an economically hostile environment for both UK and US HE, the 'for-profit' HE supplier might thrive not only by being absolutely lean and mean but also by cherry-picking from the traditional HEIs the vocational degrees market which often underpins the economics of offering the broader range of Liberal Education courses. Complementing the rather gloomy 2003 Duderstadt & Womack book on US public HEIs cited earlier is an upbeat one on the fast-growing 'for-profit', commercial sector of US HE (as opposed to the public system, or the charitable/'not-for-profit' private HEIs): R.S.Ruch, 2003, *Higher Ed., Inc: the Rise of the For-profit University*, The Johns Hopkins University Press. The tale is of almost $5b equity capital being raised in less than a decade, creating a 10% share of the $750b HE annual turn-over; and of a utilitarian, no-frills customer-oriented and business-like approach to delivering vocational HE (and certainly not messing about with an expensive loss-leader like research or indulging the faculty/academics with the inefficient luxury of tenure!). So, is the for-profit sector merely 'Drive-Thru U' or 'McEducation'? Or, within a richly diversified and massive HE system, is it just different, its mission being to cater for mature students wanting to 'get in, get out, get a job' and not needing the lavish campus infrastructure of social and sporting facilities for 'finding themselves'? It is not surprising that this for-profit sector has been lobbying (not, so far, with any great success) for the speedy adoption of WTO/GATS proposals for the liberalisation of trade in services as now broadly achieved in goods, thereby threatening the public or semi-public monopoly that is the delivery of HE in Europe, in the UK, and (to a lesser extent) in the USA.

There is alas interesting material on 'for-profit' HE and on competition, marketisation and globalisation within HE to be found at the web-site for 'The Futures Project: Policy for Higher Education in a Changing World', based at Brown University (www.futuresproject.org). There are some 4600 'for-profit' post-secondary education institutions in the USA, amounting to almost half of the total at c9650 (the other half being divided almost equally between public and private non-profit). Only some 730 of these 4600, however, are degree-granting, and they are out-numbered by c3850 degree-granting public and private non-profit competitors. If 78% of undergraduates are at public HEIs, and 16% at private non-profit HEIs, only 6% are at 'for-profits' – and, of these, a mere 1% are at 4-year HEIs (1995/96 figures): so, not much of a threat on the quantity front to traditional HEI! Deeper analysis shows that the 'for-profits' cater mainly for students in their thirties who need to bolt on a vocational degree to their work experience, that their competitive edge lies in cutting costs while efficiently and adaptively serving their market niche, and that they do fully comply with accreditation requirements (they are not an inferior product) and hence their students can receive Federal and State financial aid. Traditional 18-22 undergraduate HEIs may, however, really have something to fear if ever the 'for-profits' expanded beyond their 30-35 niche, assuming the 18-22 market is more interested in course content than campus community, in efficiency of course delivery than ease of campus drinking...

Further Papers by Newman & Couturier ('The New Competitive Arena: Market Forces Invade the Academy', 2001; and 'Trading Public Good in the Higher Education Market', 2002) explore the increasingly competitive nature of US HE as State-by-State cartels break down and hence as the system is steadily de-regulated. Such competition manifests itself in the aggressive use of merit aid to recruit the best qualified students, in students acting more like consumers, in the growth of 'for-profits', and in the provision of on-line distance-learning provision; all in all, the creation of a market-place in HE and 'a fundamentally changed climate' for HEIs, one of greater complexity and niching, one demanding a firmer grip on cost-control and a better management of teaching quality, one requiring a willingness to tackle 'the long advance of academic arteriosclerosis'. The 'for-profits' present a competitive threat not in terms of their overall quantity of students but in terms of their being able 'to cherry-pick the 'profitable' parts of the enterprise', lucrative vocational course in areas of business and school-teaching which hitherto have been used 'as revenue sources to cross-subsidise high cost majors or courses [the sciences], faculty scholarship [research], or community service [adult/continuing education]'.

Newman & Couturier predict that, 'given an absence of careful planning, traditional universities and colleges are also likely to move, a small step at a time, in a direction that brings them closer to the activities and philosophies of the for-profit institutions' (or at least they will become more 'for revenue' even if not strictly 'for-profit'), and the risk is that thereby they 'will lose the independence of mind and action that is so essential for the functioning of a free society'. And the 'careful planning' they recommend requires traditional HEIs 'to think in radically new terms', 'to ask hard questions', to engage one another in serious discussion about the structure and future of higher education', 'to define the institution's niche', to engender a campus-wide entrepreneurial spirit', and to improve teaching quality: in short, to place the emphasis on 'responsiveness, flexibility, speed - attributes not typically ascribed to the academy'. Here Newman & Couturier are preaching essentially the same message as Michael Shattock, the UK's one-man answer to the USA's 'The Futures Project', has advocated and practised for two decades and more during his time as Registrar (Cheif Operating Officer) at the University of Warwick, and as neatly encapsulated in his 2003 *Managing Successful Universities* (Open University Press/McGraw-Hill); see also Burton R. Clark, 1998, *Creating Entrepreneurial Universities* (IAU Press).

See also on the 'for-profits': J. Sperling & R.W. Tucker, 1997, *For-Profit Higher Education*, Transaction Publishers; R.L. Lenington, 1996, *Managing Higher Education as a Business*, ACE/Oryx Press; F.E Baldeston, 1995, *Managing Today's University*, Jossey-Bass; Z. Karabell, 1998, *What's College For? The Struggle to Define American Higher Education*, Basic Books; and W. Tierney, 1999, *Building the Responsive Campus: Creating High Performance*

Colleges and Universities, Sage.

In summary, US HE remains just affordable to a Middle America high on debt. It has not really faced the financial pressures confronting UK HE since the early-1980s, not least because the high-profile, private, not-for-profit HEIs have been bolstered by (until recently) the hefty growth rates in their endowments. If, however, Middle America begins to feel the pinch as the economy turns, US HE will be challenged financially and politically (California's proposed 10% budget cuts for 2004/05 and the McKeon Bill of 2003/04 being a foretaste). That said, family spending on HE, as on cars and holidays, is ultimately discretionary, and the strong faith of Middle America in the value of 'Going to College' will probably mean that HE will be prioritised over other such items of family expenditure, to the general long-term continuing benefit of US HE. In the UK, however, the shift to that willingness to pay towards HE, as opposed to expecting its provision as a virtually free public good, will take a generation and, in the meanwhile, the HEIs will suffer accordingly. And the British will not be alone in having to cope with this inevitable Americanisation of HE: it is a trend already underway in Australia and New Zealand, probably rather less so in Canada, and firmly 'on the agenda' for Ireland and Japan, and even perhaps for France... (At the time of going to print, however, the concept of any variability in the level of tuition fees charged across HEIs is repellent to many Labour MPs, who fear this 'marketisation' and even 'Americanisation' of HE. The Government is holding firm and the rebels failed by 28 votes at the amendment stage of the third reading on 31 March to get the concept of variability removed from the Bill...).

For a definitive history of student financial aid in the USA, see R.H. Wilkinson, forthcoming (2004, Vanderbilt University Press), *Dollars for Scholars: Aiding Students, Buying Students in American History and Modern Society*; see also John Douglass, forthcoming (2004, Vanderbilt University Press), *The Social Contract of Public Universities*.

5

ACCESS

So, if 'Middle America' can still afford to go to the HE ball, can Cinderalla 'Poor America'? Hearn, in Chapter 11 of Paulsen & Smart, considers the issue of access and social mobility in US HE, and, in making the following key points, not only echoes both Kane and also McPherson & Schapiro but awards US HE only a 'could do better' assessment:

- Lower-income youngsters now want to go to college as much as anyone else; entering HE is 'the norm across all income groups'; there is no longer an aspiration or expectation gap.
- The participation rate of such lower-income students has 'improved dramatically' (42% of the lowest-income quartile young entered HE in 1982; 53% in 1992 – progress which is 'noteworthy and heartening', and which (allowing for problems in comparing the US income-group oranges with the UK SEG apples) seems better than UK HE achieves (at c10% – although that 10% may not be as feeble as it seems in that some aspects of UK FE activity need to be counted as the equivalent of US HE taking place in the community colleges as the usual supplier of HE to such lower-income students).
- But the enrolment gap between the low-income group students and others has grown; they may be going to college more, but their better-off peers are going in even greater numbers.
- And the gap between expecting to go to college and actually enrolling is 'far greater among lower-income students than others, and has grown since 1982'; they want to go but are less likely to be able to do so than their better-off counterpart, and are less likely than their peers a decade before.
- Nor is this expectation/enrolment-participation gap a function of factors besides family income.
- The 'massive investment' in SFA has clearly facilitated access, but in recent years the policy shift away from needs-based SFA towards loans and merit-aid has disadvantaged low-income groups. The SFA system has become less equitable, since loan-aid is less fair than grant-aid and especially so where 'the financial aid system has

become more complex and difficult to understand'; 'current aid programs seem too complex, too diluted, and too modest'; 'lower-income students are more vulnerable than ever'. As Kane puts it: 'low-income students, who are particularly price sensitive, seem to be losing out'; while McPherson & Schapiro comment that 'increases in net cost over time lead to decreases in enrollment rates for lower-income students...no evidence that increases in net cost inhibited enrolment for more affluent students...[hence] policies that call for cross-sudsidization of students – richer students paying a substantial share of educational and general costs with these revenues supporting discounts for lower-income students – makes sense from the viewpoint of economic efficiency'. Easier, more user-friendly SFA procedures would help, but above all the value of the Pell Grant (down by 20% in real terms since 1980; maximum value now $4K compared with c$7K needed to restore its 1975 buying-power) needs to be hugely increased: exactly the same access issue as identified in chapter 1 above for UK HE.

- But the 'access' issue in HE is not solely about money...Lesley Pugsley in 'Choice or Chance: The University Challenge – How Schools Reproduce and Produce Social Capital in the Choice Process' (chapter 11 of Geoffrey Walford, 2003, *British Public Schools: Research on Policy and Practice*. London: Woburn Press/Cass) argues that young people's choices about university entry are dependent on 'class-based competencies', with the well-placed independent school pupil having his/her existing cultural/social/family advantages reinforced by the expertise of the well-resourced school's 'commitment to university and careers guidance' in providing 'the very best practice in terms of higher-education guidance and support'. Such pupils become 'privileged choosers' amongst the bewildering offerings of UK HEIs, aided and abetted as they are by the school's determination to place its products in the upper end of the range of universities by being highly structured and organised about HE applications and also by creating and utilising an extensive network of contacts, especially among Oxbridge colleges. (Of course, through getting its output into high status HEIs the ever-increasing private school fees are partly justified to the paying parent.)

- Similarly, research in the USA (the San Diego 'Advancement via Individual Determination' project, AVID) is cited by Pugsley as underlining the value of schools giving more help to lower social class and ethnic minority students and their families with the college entry process (Mehan, H., et al, 1999, *Constructing School Success*, Cambridge: CUP). Thus, 'a lifeline in the form of a well-structured programme of higher education guidance' is advocated in order that such youngsters are not left 'to drown in the whirlpool of university choices' and in order to achieve access policies which are 'truly inclusive across the spectrum of social class'. But who will pay for it? – the Government keen to hit its 50% target? Or the State schools anxious to perform in league tables? Or the HEIs desperate not to fall foul of the White Paper's proposed 'Access Tsar'?

McPherson & Schapiro give 'freshman enrollment' 1994 figures by income background across institutional types: the two lowest-income groups (up to $30K pa) of the six sent just 6% to a private university compared with 22% for the richest group ($200K+) and 13% for the upper-middle group ($100-200K); at the public university the figures were 25%, 25% and 28%; and at the 2-year publics/community colleges 87%, 9% and 14% (the private university caters for only 6% of US HE students, the public university for 20%, the community colleges for 31%; the rest are in private and public 4-year colleges). They comment: '...the probability of a student's attending a four-year private college or university depends critically on his or her parents' income...Perhaps the most striking finding is that 41% of upper-income and 47% of the richest students attend a university (private or public), compared with only 13.5% of lower-income students' (pp 44/45). Kane records that 90% of those young people from families with an income above $90K go to HE, compared with 40% for below $13K families (1992/93 data): 'College enrollment apparently differs dramatically by family income...'

Scott Thomas (Institute of Higher Education, University of Georgia), in an important Paper on 'Globalization, College Participation, and Socioeconomic Mobility' delivered at a Spring 2003 IHE Seminar, discussed the 'stratification of opportunity' within US HE and noted how some HEIs offer a greater personal rate of return for their Liberal Arts graduates and how 'access to the colleges that provide the greatest benefits is unequal and this inequality [is] problematically tied with family socio-economic status': '...colleges, being institutions of the dominant class structure, tend to offer benefits in proportion to the cultural capital students bring to their campuses...Prestigious institutions more greatly magnify the effects of one's cultural capital than do institutions of lesser prestige...High prestige institutions therefore might be understood as superchargers of one's cultural capital...' (See also Scott Thomas, 'Longer-term economic effects of college selectivity and control', in

Research in Higher Education, 44 (3), 2003.) D.W. Breneman (University of Virginia) at the same Seminar commented: 'The era of low-tuition public higher education is coming to a close, which vitiates the ability of Pell Grants to ensure access. Tuition tax credits do little for the poor, and loans at the level required to meet rising tuition and related costs will be seen as prohibitive by many potential students' [or at least those from 'Poor America'].

Finally, J. V. Welman (2002) explores the significant role of the community colleges in being the dominant route for 'Poor America' to access HE, especially via the progression to a 4-year HEI ('State Policy and Community College – Baccalaurate Transfer', Institute for Higher Education Policy, at *www.highereducation.org*). Roughly 25% of those students commencing full-time at a 2-year community college transfer to 4-year HEIs, and c70% of them then go on to graduate (cf c65% overall completion from 4-year HEIs, with in excess of 90% at the 'highly selective' ones, but fading away to less than 45% (sic) at some public HEIs: see, for example, the *Fiske Guide to Colleges 2004*, which lists some 500 HEIs and ranks 44 'Best Buys' according to the balance of price and quality while warning that 'price and quality do not always go hand in hand'!). Interestingly for the UK as the White Paper contemplates 2-year 'Foundation Degrees' as the economical way to expand HE provision, Welman notes in relation to the USA: 'The 2/4 community college-baccalaurate transfer function is one of the most important issues in higher education because its success (or failure) is central to many dimensions of state higher education performance, including access, equity, affordability, cost effectiveness, degree productivity, and quality. States that have strong 2/4 transfer performance will have lower state appropriations per degree [HE in CCs is cheap: faculty salaries are lower, infrastructure is less fancy, there is no expensive research going on, and the staff/student ratio is likely to be less generous...]. They will also do a better job of translating access into success and of reducing achievement disparities that prevent low-income and minority students from obtaining the baccalaurate degree.' (p 3). The California HE model is a prime example.

Hence, UK and US HE policies may potentially converge in at least this one respect (if not – yet – in relation to 'deregulation' and high-fees/high-aid), and they may soon each increasingly utilise the 2-year Associate/Foundation Degree route: 'Given the current growth in postsecondary enrolment demand (the so-called baby-boom echo), coupled with constraints on state funding, more states are planning to use community colleges as a low-cost alternative to expanding their four-year campuses. The pressure on community college-baccalaurate transfer performance will be especially acute in the Sunbelt states: California is projecting a 21% increase (from 1999 to 2010) in high school graduates, the majority of whom are expected to go on to a community college; Arizonia, a 34% increase; Florida, 26%; North Carolina, 20%; and Texas, 12%.' (p 4). Welman calls for 'a comprehensive, integrated approach to transfer policy' in order to 'energize 2/4 transfer performance' as 'an effective tool for diversity and mobility within higher education' (p 45).

Mission Drift

Moreover, also at the UGA IHE gathering Kenneth Redd (National Association of Student Financial Aid Administrators) observed that surveys showed 'colleges and universities are turning away from their traditional mission of using their grant funds to provide access and educational opportunity for poor families. Instead...[they] are using their institutional grants as marketing 'tools' to attract the 'best and brightest' undergraduates to their campuses...[which means that] If the growth of negotiation [over the SFA package] on college campuses is indeed a 'price war', those students and families with the sharpest negotiating skills and demonstrated academic abilities appear to be in the best position to fight and win it. The ultimate losers in this conflict may be those from low-income families who do not have the skills or academic records to keep pace.' (See Redd, NASFAA Journal of Student Financial Aid, 32 (2) 24-36; and Redd, 'Discounting Toward Disaster', USA Group Foundation 'New Agenda Series', 3 (2) 2000, www.usagroup.com.)

Nor, as Donald Heller (Penn State) noted at the Seminar, do the growing number of State Merit Scholarship Programs necessarily alter the picture: for example, Georgia's 'Helping Outstanding Students Educationally' (HOPE) scheme funnels tax-dollars from the State lottery (played disproportionately by low-income folk) overwhelmingly to the students of middle-income and higher-income families who earn a 'HOPE' for HE by doing well at high school; such schemes are decidedly 'regressive' and 'pernicious' (some States use their share of the national tobacco litigation settlement where, again, cigarette consumption is skewed towards low-income groups!). See also Heller, D. E. (2001) *The states and public higher education policy: Affordability, access, and accountability.* Baltimore: The Johns Hopkins University Press; and Heller's *Condition of Access: Higher Education for Lower Income Students.* 2002, Westport CT: ACE/Praeger. In the latter it is stressed that: 'Financial aid does not even pay half the cost of attending the lowest-priced colleges in America for lower-income undergraduates' (p 38).

Thus, a 'Poor America' family needs to make a greater effort to allow the student to attend college than does the middle-income or upper-income family where there is less inhibition about incurring debt to finance HE as a life-investment. Moreover, as already noted, need-aid for 'Poor America' has lost ground to merit-aid for 'Middle America': the former growing by only 90% or so in constant dollars 1982-1999, the latter by some 4.5 times (p 66). Similarly, the 1990s tax credits schemes favour the middle and upper income groups in terms of their ability to use them as part of their saving arrangements for funding college: a 'highly inefficient' policy (p 88). Improving lower-income group college enrolment and degree completion rates will involve not only enhanced SFA packages, but also 'Pre-college Outreach and Early Intervention Programs' (Chapter 6) and 'Support Strategies for Disadvantaged Students' (Chapter 7) – the latter involving remedial courses for almost a third of first-year students (especially in maths).

Gordon C. Winston (Williams College) in an article on 'Why Colleges Pay Wages to their Students' (*Chronicle of Higher Education*, 28/11/03, B 20) explores 'peer effects' (clever, lively, committed students encourage each other to strive); the quality of the student is 'an important input to its production [educational quality]' and, via tuition fee discounting ('a hot bidding war for scarce top-student peer talent'), it can be bought just like good faculty, fancy buildings, top-notch lab equipment. Thus, at Williams College the cost of the educational package is $75K p.a., the sticker-price is $34K, and the average fees paid $24K (giving '$51,000 a year in subsidies – an implicit wage'). But such price competition via merit aid, scholarships and fee discounting means the low-income student loses out: '… colleges are battling to retain or improve their peer quality at the expense of their previous dedication to equal opportunity. Cutting prices and offering merit aid to attract students with high peer quality who are, as often as not, affluent – limits how much colleges can pay poor students of equal quality who must also receive need-based financial aid… in the rush to compete for students offering peer quality, will colleges freeze out growing numbers of students with far greater financial needs?' Clearly, in so far as UK HE may yet steadily move closer to the US HE model, there would presumably be concern that any use of merit aid aimed at maximising peer quality was not at the expense of financing truly needs-blind recruitment/admission policies aimed at achieving equity in access.

Another valuable insight is 'Access Denied: Restoring the Nation's Commitment to Equal Educational Opportunity', a 2001 Report from the Advisory Committee on Student Financial Assistance (www.ed.gov/ACFSA). Low-income family (up to \$25K pa) participation in HE lags behind that of high-income families (\$75K+) by 32%, and has barely changed over three decades (as also in the UK); non-completion rates are similarly skewed against 'Poor America'; only 6 % of students 'with the lowest socio-economic status' earn a bachelor degree compared with 40% 'with the highest SES' and 20% for the middle quartile SESs: 'Such policies are not only inequitable but also economically inefficient at any level – federal, state, or institutional'. The gap is set to widen as the HEIs increase tuition fees and as the value of Federal SFA declines relative to general consumer prices let alone those above-inflation increasing HE costs, and as States and HEIs continue the steady shift away from financial-need SFA to merit-need SFA: in short, 'an access crisis' looms as the system contends with 'record levels of unmet need'. As in the UK, 'SES remains a very powerful barrier to attending college at all', and 'unmet need' can still counter progress arising from improving schooling for lower SES groups: 97% of the overlapping highest achievement/highest SES quartiles go to college, 78% of the highest achievement/lowest SES, and 77% - 36% for the lowest achievement/highest-lowest SES quartiles (ie. one-third of poor kids of low academic achievement still get to go to college in the USA, but three-quarters of the low-achiever rich kids also get to go).

User-friendly SFA forms and ever-better publicity will help, but not if in the last analysis there remains an unmet need gap as a result of lack of finance for SFA. The USA, declares the Report, must 'reinstate the access goal' that 'all academically prepared, low-income students could attend either a two-year or four-year institution full-time' as 'the nation's access benchmark'. Thus, for example, the Federal Pell Grant would need to more than double to regain its 1975/76 buying-power; States would need to redirect SFA as need-based rather than merit-based; HEIs would have once again to concentrate their SFA on making HE more accessible for low-income America rather than more affordable for middle-income America…in short, the 1965-80 constructive partnership of Federal, State and HEI shared HE policy-making needs to be resurrected. What chance?

Access: UK v US

How then does the US access picture compare with the UK? As already noted, even if many of the access issues and problems are comparable (family aspirations/expectations, poor schooling, social/cultural capital, the perceived alien 'middle-classness' of 'prestige' universities, simply the overall amount of money available as student financial aid, the technicalities of the means-testing mechanism and the resultant balance of grants v. loans, etc), the data sets are not easily compared. US HE seems to accommodate more entrants from lower-income and SES groups than does UK HE (with FE) from the lower SEGs, but fewer of them, once admitted, then reach graduation. In both cases, however, these students are less likely to go to college than their peers from higher-income/SES and SEG groups, and when they do get into HE are then to be found concentrated in the less-prestigious HEIs and especially in the community colleges (as the equiv-alent of the HE and much of the FE taking place within the UK FE sector). But 'Poor America' is perhaps less likely to be at the Ivy League HEI than the students from lower-income families or SEGs IV & V are to be study-ing at low-fee Oxbridge; the former, however, will probably be a little more readily found in the likes of, say, Berkeley as a top public than in, say, Stanford as a top private across the Bay.

If, however, the 'Poor America' student does make it to the top private, it may well be more affordable, given high levels of financial aid (espe-cially by way of the HEI's grants) and despite high tuition fees, than Oxford, Cambridge, Imperial and UCL for his/her counterpart in the UK, given the UK emphasis on loans and despite low fees. On completion rates US HE, as already noted, looks weak: the National Centre for Public Policy and Higher Education annual report for 2002 (summary at www.highereducation.org) records few State HE systems where a major-ity of full-time students complete undergraduate studies within 5 years; in no State do more than 70% of students graduate within 5 or even 6 years (cf the UK well-above OECD norms figure at c80% completion within the prescribed 3 or 4 year degree course length, even if some critics might claim that HEIs are 'dumbing down' to achieve the pass rate and point out that some UK HEIs do now have a non-completion rate approaching 40%). As for community colleges, the preserve of 'Poor America', in half the 50 or so States more than half of students do not return for year two (attrition rates for HND courses in the UK FEIs are also greater than for degree courses in the HEIs). In this regard at least, US HE is closer to the European model of high access to year one, but with a high attrition rate and/or high non-completion rate (or at least a painfully slow, and economically inefficient, completion rate).

As Thomas Weko argues, however, it may be better to have an open, flexible, easy/wide access HE system (even at the risk of higher non-com-pletion rates, c35% for the USA to the UK's c20% and the OECD average at just under 25%: NB Italy and France at c40% compared to Japan at 5%!), than a crowded-elite system less accommodating to non-traditional stu-dents – and especially if there is no stigma attached to not completing college (cf. the UK use of 'wastage' or 'drop-out' rates until fairly recently): 'New Dogs and Old Tricks. What can the UK teach the US about University Education?', British Council/AfPP Report, March 2004 (crll.gcal.ac.uk/events/SemWeko). In short, it is a public policy trade-off of attaching greater emphasis to maximising opportunity within the HE system rather than to economic efficiency. Again, back to the fundamental question of access to what, for whom and for how long; and to a supplementary question of access at whose expense.

Politics, Politics

The politics of affordability of HE for 'Middle America' have during the 1990s trumped the politics of access to HE for 'Poor America', which is not surprising given the relative voting power of the two constituencies: a scenario potentially echoed in the UK where in response to New Labour's White Paper and its proposed £3K pa tuition fee for 'Middle England' the Conservative Party has focussed on affordability, initially asserting that it would avoid the need to increase fees by reducing the size of the HE system (and hence its accessibility to 'Poor England') as a means of saving money. (Nick Barr of the LSE calculated this would involve a loss of c80K places in a total undergraduate full-time student population of some 1m; while the Institute of Fiscal Studies described the policy as 'uniformly regressive' and saw a loss of some 50K HE places.) In fact, Callender in Hayton & Paczuska (as cited in chapter 1 above) argues that, since New Labour came to power in 1997, this same political process of accessibility yielding to affordability has happened also in the UK: 'socially regressive' changes have 'prioritised the expansion in higher education at the expanse of widening access and increasing the representation of lower class groups whose loss of state assistance was used to fund higher education expansion in all classes' (p 85): Hutchings in Chapter 8 of Archer, as cited in chapter 1, makes the same point.

This is, indeed, all something of a shame if the results of a California survey undertaken by Flacks & Thomas are to be believed ('Among Affluent Students, a Culture of Disengagement', *The Chronicle of Higher Education*, 27/11/1998): 'Students whose parents are highly educated and affluent are more likely to drink, use drugs, and party frequently, and are less likely to spend time studying, than are less-privileged students...The culture of disengagement embraced by many of today's advantaged students seems rooted in a pervasive belief that the main purpose of going to college is economic...[Those students] whose families have made sacrifices so that they can go to college, or who have struggled themselves to pursue an education... want not simply to get a degree, but to expand their intellectual horizons – to obtain the means to fulfil their potential as people and citizens, not just to improve their marketability...'

Clearly echoes here of the current UK debate stimulated by the White Paper's 'Access Regulator' (aka 'OffToff'!) proposal expressing concern about top HEIs supposedly admitting students solely on 'achievement' measured by high grades already gained at 'a good school' (independent or 'posh comp') as opposed to (slightly?) lower grades achieved at a less well-resourced school ('a bog-standard comprehensive', to borrow a phrase from a Government spokesperson!) being used to assess 'potential' for HE. In effect, a nudge towards a kind of 'affirmative action' recruitment/admissions policy for UK HEIs that would favour applicants from 'poor postcodes'; and a nudge given further emphasis by the work commissioned from Professor Schwartz (Brunel University) on the UK HE application process.

Already the media speculation over the Schwarz interim/draft recommendations (April 2004, *www.admissions-review.org.uk*) has begun: might any such 'social engineering' (perhaps in effect 'dumbing-down') be challenged as illegal 'positive discrimination' under the Human Rights Act by an aggrieved applicant from a well-resourced private school rejected by an elite university in favour of a seemingly less well-qualified applicant from the wrong side of the scholastic tracks but from just the right postcode (zip-code)? Yet what of research which suggests that the student (with similar A-level grades) from the less privileged State school may well, in fact, perform better academically at university – see the HEPI Report on 'Widening Participation and Access' (Executive Summary, para. 23) at *www.hepi.ac.uk*, 'Articles' Page; as echoed in the Schwarz initial report at para. 4.2 and in its Appendix 4 which refers to, and indeed commends to the attention of the HEI when determining its admissions policy, a 'rigorous and robust' HEFCE paper on 'Schooling Effects on Higher Education Achievement' (HEFCE, 2003/32) that concludes: 'Students from independent schools appear to do less well than students from other schools, all other things being equal. The size of this effect varies between the equivalent of one and four A-level points [eg. a State school 24 point, ABC entrant might in Finals match the performance of a private school 28 point, AAB entrant]...For the most highly selective HEIs, students from LEA [State] schools do consistently better than similar students from independent schools.'

The Schwarz team, however, has taken legal advice (set out in its Appendix 5) and it shows as it treads carefully (para. B25): each HEI must reach its own decision on the vexed issue of discrimination law ('This appendix is **not** a substitute for legal advice...'!). That said, it seems that:

- while a HEI need not give reasons for rejecting an applicant and even if the court will not trespass on academic judgement in selecting amongst applicants, the HEI clearly must not contravene discrimination laws on race, sex, disability, religion, sexual orientation, and (from December 2006) age;
- but some 'differential treatment' may still be allowed under the Human Rights Act and its incorporation into English Law of the European Convention on Human Rights if it can be 'objectively justified' as pursuing 'a legitimate aim and is reasonably necessary and proportionate to the aim pursued';
- and such an aim 'of redressing a pre-existing situation of inequality' could indeed lawfully be 'improving access to HE for disadvantaged or under-represented groups';
- although that 'differential treatment' should not be a simplistic 'broad brush' approach, treating 'one applicant automatically more or less favourably by virtue of his or her background, school or college';
- instead 'applicants should be assessed as individuals', there should be 'holistic assessment' ('a broad range of additional information, including relevant skills and contextual factors as well as academic achievement...');
- and, by the way, a HEI may well see it as 'a legitimate aim' to ensure 'a diverse student community' (crucially, the Schwarz Group 'is aware of a recent decision by the US Supreme Court upholding a university's "compelling interest in obtaining the educational benefits that flow from a diverse student body."...').

All in all, and assuming the Schwarz 'recommendations' do not end up as a damp-squib and are picked up by the OFFA, there is not much comfort here for Middle England, having expensively educated its young at private schools, soon finding its university applicants given, seemingly lawfully, subtle 'differential treatment' by way of 'holistic assessment' in the name of recruiting 'a diverse student body'. The Schwarz 'recommendations', if given bite through OFFA, will surely do wonders for the recruitment campaigns of US Ivy League HEIs already fishing for diversified student talent in the UK, and just possibly also for the UK's only truly private/independent Liberal Arts college in the form of the University of Buckingham: but all, Middle England will discover, at tuition fee levels dramatically higher than those proposed in the 2004 Higher Education Bill! Thus, Middle England faces a pincer movement: the elite HEIs, even after the introduction of higher (but, sadly, capped too low) tuition fees from 2006, are likely to sacrifice uneconomic UK/EU undergraduate places for higher fee overseas students and what UK/EU places remain at the elites will be partially (on the basis of sophisticated and legally safe 'holistic assessment') reallocated to 'under-represented groups' at the expense of private school and 'posh post-code' applicants (with, if the HEFCE research is to be believed, even an improvement in the degree profiles of the elite HEIs!). No wonder that the Conservative opposition in the run-up to an election senses votes in challenging the concept of the 'Access Tsar', while being confused as to whether to oppose modestly higher tuition fees which at first sight hit the Middle England pocket but are nothing to what awaits if their university age children are driven out of the UK elites into the US Ivy League. And no wonder that the civil rights lawyers sense money as the HEIs are warned of the need to have their access policies vetted, and as the Independent Schools Council doubtlessly amasses its fighting fund for a test case on just how 'positive' or 'affirmative' such 'differential treatment' can lawfully be in any 'holistic assessment' admissions criteria aimed at creating an 'objectively justified' public benefit of 'a diverse student community' (and it will be an expensive test case: County Court, Court of Appeal, House of Lords, and then off to the Strasbourg Court of Human Rights). In the meanwhile, the 'OffToff' and the Schwarz Group's 'Outline of Model Institutional Admissions Policy' (Appendix 6) will do nothing for independent schools' overall pupil recruitment and especially retention in the Sixth Form, particularly at a time when the schools face an OFT investigation into an alleged fee-fixing cartel, are having to do a lot more by way of bursaries to demonstrate their public benefit under the impending tightening up of charity law, and are encountering (some might think rather belatedly) hints of real consumer resistance to the endless annual fee hikes... One may safely predict a speedy 'review' of the OFFA if there is a change of Government in 2006, and perhaps a more rational Conservative Party policy on higher tuition fees as the least unpalatable of a wide range of higher education evils for Middle England!

Thus, the question becomes: Access to what, access for whom, and indeed for how long? Is there much point in Chuck, or Henri his French cousin or Kurt his German pen-friend, going to college if they are not likely to stay the course, and, even if the taxpayer funds them less generously than a generation ago, could not the same public money have been better spent elsewhere in the public services? (See Alison Wolf's *Does Education Matter?*, as cited in chapter 1; and also (forthcoming, RoutledgeFalmer/Taylor & Francis, 2004) Tapper & Palfreyman

Understanding Mass Higher Education: Comparative Perspectives on Access; on the legal implications of the 'OffToff' see N. Saunders (forthcoming Vol 16 of Education and the Law, 2004) 'Widening Access to Higher Education – the Limits of Positive Action') Moreover, in terms of 'access to what?', it is a sad indictment of UK HE, and indeed of HE systems generally, that impenetrable mystery surrounds just what is to be defined as 'quality' within the undergraduate educational experience. There is no agreed standard, say, as to the optimum (or even bare minimum) amount of written work a student should produce in earning a degree or as to the appropriate size of seminars and classes for ensuring adequate student-academic interaction, conveniently leaving the HE industry with virtually total freedom to minimise expenditure by steadily curtailing the teaching input but while seemingly never, of course, compromising quality. It remains unclear whether quality across HE is best achieved, maintained and enhanced by relying on the integrity of the academic profession, on a quality-control management hierarchy within the HEI, on quality-regulation by some external inspecting agency, on the need in appropriate cases for accreditation of the degree course with the relevant professional body, or on empowering the student as a fee-paying consumer to counter a strong tendency towards a producer-orientation in HEIs.

Certainly, one suspects that Government as the provider of decreasing levels of funding per student probably does not really want to know how little the taxpayer might be getting as value-for-money by way of a 'conversation' between teacher and taught in the form of routine, frequent, sustained and marked written-work and seminar-participation, and, in the context of a HE policy driven more by maximising the quantity of students admitted rather than the quality of degrees achieved, would not thank its quality-monitoring agency for delving too deeply and rigorously into the hard detail of course teaching contact-hours and assessment requirements as opposed to concentrating on the nebulous jargon of 'learning outcomes' and the like. (On quality see Roger Brown, 2004, *Quality Assurance in Higher Education: The UK Experience since 1992*, RoutledgeFalmer / Taylor & Francis.)

6

CONCLUSIONS

If US HE imposes higher (and increasingly high) tuition fees than the UK HE system now at some £1125 pa (or probably by 2006 at £3000 pa), does it still remain affordable for 'Middle America' and at the same time accessible to 'Poor America'? If so, it is a rare example of a socialist redistribution mechanism that actually works: the few rich pay hefty fees that are used partly to discount the sticker-price for the middle-income many and even eliminate it for the poor few, while also ensuring that the USA has the lion's share of global-class HEIs (whether mainly private Ivy League or the fewer 'public Ivies' as flagship campuses). Higher fee levels certainly, whether at the public HEI or at the private HEI; probably still affordable; world-class HEIs undeniably (Princeton, Harvard, Yale, MIT, Stanford, Berkeley, , Columbia, and (?) half-a-dozen others).

The bit, however, which has a question-mark over it must be the access aspect: see chapter 5. Even if access is losing out to affordability in the US (as, arguably, also in the UK), the questions are: a) whether the US high-fee, mixed-economy, public-private HE system recruits more of the poor than the UK's low-fee, 'nationalised-industry' HE system, and b) keeps them safely through to graduation; and c) whether the mega-fee Ivy League US HEIs are as or more accessible to the lower-income/SES US student than Oxford & Cambridge, Imperial, and UCL are to the appropriately academically-qualified lower-income/lower-SEG UK applicants. Referring back to the data in chapter 1 above, the answers seem to be: a = yes, (more of the US poor do indeed get to go to (or, rather, at least to start) college than their UK counterparts); b = not necessarily (the non-completion rate for all students, and especially those from low-income families, is high in the US HE system, and higher than at present in the UK – even if in the UK students from low-income families are much more likely to 'drop-out' of HE than their middle-class counterparts); and c = uncertain (although once the 'Poor America' student is admitted to a top US public, and perhaps especially to a top private, HEI staying there to graduation is probably as likely as at Oxford and may well be at less personal cost by way of debt, given grant levels at Princeton et al, than for the poor Brit attending one of his/her own country's top HEIs on the inadequate level of Government subsidised loan).

Clearly, however, more work is needed to compare accurately the c10-15% of lower-income family students at, say, Oxford (measured by the number means-tested at a sample of colleges to have all of the University tuition fee paid for them, and hence indicating a parental income of some £20K/$30K or less) - and preferably also at, say, Cambridge, Imperial and UCL - with the student numbers from the corresponding low-income groups at, say, Stanford, Berkeley, Princeton, MIT, Columbia, and Harvard... See the US data quoted from Wolf in chapter 1, where, seemingly and allowing for the problem of comparing 'lower' with 'low', perhaps these 'highly selective' universities' do not recruit as widely from 'Poor America' (the 'low-income' band is up to 20K in 1997 $s) as Oxford manages from 'Poor(ish) England' (where 'lower-income', as noted above, is up to 20K in 2003 £s, or c$30K); and recall from chapter 1 Halsey's untested 'important cross-national hypothesis' of 'narrowed' recruitment at 'the most prestigious universities': could Oxford, for once, actually be doing something right in terms of 'the politics of access'?! As Stevens (see citation below) notes: 'In the autumn of 2000, Oxford took 42.5 per cent of students from the seven per cent of students at [fee-paying] independent schools, and 48.2 per cent from [free] state schools, which overall have 93 per cent of students. Yale took 32 per cent [and Harvard also the same proportion] of its students from the prep and country day schools which two per cent of American children attend. And 61 per cent of its students came from the public schools (state schools) and parochial (Catholic) schools which 98 per cent of American students attend.'

The US Century Foundation has recently (April, 2004) published a Report ('Left Behind: Unequal Opportunity in Higher Education', www.tcf.org) which records 75% of students at the top 150 HEIs as being from the wealthiest socio-economic quartile, and only 3% from the poorest; in other words, a student at an elite US HEI is 25 times more likely to be from a well-off family than from a poor family. (See also R.D. Kahlenberg (ed), *America's Untapped Resource: Low-Income Students in Higher Education*, 2004 forthcoming, The Century Foundation.) As noted already, the UK elite HEIs achieve greater access for the poorer student (perhaps because the school system is, despite its weaknesses, less uneven across the country and the socio-economic groups than is the case in the US), and are under increasing political pressure to broaden access further (informal pressure at present via the Schwarz Group's 'recommendations' as discussed above; perhaps soon as pressure by way of a strict condition of charging higher tuition fees as imposed by the OFFA, also as discussed above). As ever in this exploration of the economics and social equity of HE, whether in the US system or in the UK system (or indeed across Europe – see Tapper & Palfreyman on comparative access to HE as cited earlier, 2004 forthcoming), we come back to a political balancing of access to: what form of HE (full-time, part-time, flexibility between the two; residential, live-at-home/commuter, distance-learning), where (public, private; 'elite' HEI, 'ordinary' HEI, community college), for how long (the full-length first degree or a shortened version; non-completion rates), for whom (fairness of access for males/females, ethnic minorities, socio-economic groups, rural/urban dwellers, mature entrants), why (for social, cultural/Liberal Arts, citizenship, or economic/vocational purposes), and (crucially for our purposes) at whose expense (Government/taxpayer, student/family, employer 'golden hellos', alumni donations). No country seems able to, or perhaps can afford to, achieve a perfect balance and the emphasis changes over time as to why and how HE is funded and by whom, what type of HE and HEI are provided (or even allowed), how flexible the system is, its accountability and efficiency, whether non-completion is an issue, and so on… For example, in the USA over recent decades equity of access for racial groups seems to have been in greater focus than that for low-income socio-economic groups, in contrast to the concentration at present in the UK on access to HE generally and to elite HEIs specifically for working-class students.

Deregulation: Opportunity or Threat?

If US HE is the most extensive, diverse and well-funded in the world, and also a system where market forces are set free to the greatest degree (but not totally), what state is it in at the beginning of the new century? There is a substantial (and somewhat polemical and strident) literature labouring on its perceived defects (and especially its alleged enslavement to political correctness): for example, most recently, Stanley Aronowitz, *The Knowledge Factory: Dismantling the Corporate University and Creating True Higher Learning* (2000) and Zachary Karabell, *What's College For? The Struggle to Define American Higher Education* (1998), each building on earlier material such as Bill Readings, *The University in Ruins* (1996), Dinesh D'Souza, *Illiberal Education* (1991), Roger Kimball, *Tenured Radicals* (1989), Charles Sykes, *Profscam* (1988), and Allen Bloom, *The Closing of the American Mind: How Higher Education Has Failed Democracy and Impoverished the Souls of Today's Students* (1987). More sober and balanced assessments of the state of US HE, and of its future, are to be found in Steven Brint, *The Future of the City of Intellect: The Changing American University* (2002) and Philip G. Altbach et al, *In Defence of American Higher*

Education (2001).

Leaving aside the debate over campus political correctness and concentrating on the extent to which the marketisation of US HE can be seen as either devaluing the purity of the true university or alternatively as positively reinforcing its autonomy and diversity, we find the critics of the present delivery of HE pointing towards such alleged defects as:

- Its poor value for money as far as the taxpayer is concerned and as far as the average student at the average HEI is concerned, where complacent tenured academics interested only in their personal research are reluctant and incompetent teachers of a steadily 'dumbed-down' curriculum in increasingly over-crowded lectures and seminars to the unengaged young seeking the least demanding route through college, and where all are equally confused over just what HE is meant to be about and for (the Karabell analysis). Here the problem is an imperfect market: the producer-oriented universal, public HEIs fail to provide what skills the ordinary student seeks (or even should be given), the consumer is far from being empowered despite viewing HE as a commodity purchase (hence the recent success of the Phoenix 'for-profit' model as the no nonsense and efficient delivery of HE?).

- Its cynical corporatism whereby the average university is now merely a big-business and a mass-volume degree-mill, providing 'higher training' for students once graduated to fill lower management and technician jobs rather than for students to receive a life-enhancing higher education (the Aronowitz thesis). Here the market is working all too well: if the student and taxpayer will finance only a cheap product, that's precisely what they will get – a dumbed-down and vocational curriculum, a commodification of the academic labour force, a loss of collegiality or shared-governance within the academic profession as decision-making is centralised to 'the Administration'.

And what can be said in defence of US HE? As it happens we now have a recent edited text (Altbach, cited above) and, in the context of constant attacks on US HE for its 'inefficiency, irresponsibility, and ungovernability', it stresses the following:

- The US HE model is 'the most influential academic model in the world', simultaneously criticised within the USA while emulated and lauded abroad as a flexible and diverse 'nonsystem' compared to 'highly centralised and bureaucratic academic systems that are difficult to change and rather inflexible in the face of new circumstances' (Altbach, Chapter 1).

- US HE has become 'a mature industry' and Government is less kind to it as awkward questions are asked about the efficiency of this sizeable part of the GNP; and the industry responds by 'doing a miserable job' of answering them! It has also been slow to adjust to the economics of being a mature industry, as well as to student/customer changing expectations (convenience, service, quality, low cost) – and hence the growth of the University of Phoenix and other 'for profit' competitors in the knowledge/media industry. In short, US HE 'faces the choice between [painful] reform and [very painful] revolution' (Levine, Chapter 2). But is all this talk of crisis just so much hype? Yes, we are told in Chapter 3 (Birnbaum & Shushok) – and Henry Mintzberg is quoted: 'We glorify ourselves by describing our own age as turbulent. We live where it's at, as the saying goes, or at least we like to think we do (because that makes us feel important).In other words, what we really face are not turbulent times but overinflated egos'. In essence, US HE is in good shape; if it is in crisis, then it is no more so than it has been since 1850 or thereabouts...

- HE is a major component of 'the American dream', which in turn is 'fundamental to the American political system, survives hostility and cynicism, and underpins America's peculiar mixture of conservatism and radical populism'; and also it works as a mass, even universal, system (just as the European systems still struggle to complete the shift from expanded elite to mass – 'The biggest hindrance to the development of European universities into mass institutions is the continuing refusal by European governments, supported by the majority of academics, to allow universities to charge tuition fees and to retain these funds for their own development and use' (Trow, Chapter 5).

- HE costs are not nearly as out-of-control as the critics allege, and anyway HE, as a service-industry lacking the productivity gains to be found in the manufacturing sector of the economy, is never going to keep its cost increases only in line with RPI. Moreover, 'there is abundant evidence that much or most (but not all) of higher education is both well managed and lean, particularly given what it is being asked by society to accomplish'. (Johnston, Chapter 6.)

- Student satisfaction with HE is 'generally high'; employers 'seem to be relatively satisfied' with the graduates they get from HE (Kuh, Chapter 11).

- And the governance of HEIs is a balancing act that works, most of the time: 'the ambiguous combination of faculty governance that protects centuries-old academic privileges and practices and modern presidential and lay trustee governance that nudges the institution toward necessary accommodations to novel conditions and fiscal realities is a surprisingly good one' (Keller, Chapter 12).

'University to Uni'

Perhaps, however, Altbach et al offer us a somewhat Panglossian assessment of US HE, even if its critics exaggerate to make the point: the reality lies, as ever, somewhere in the middle, but, whatever may be the true position, it is difficult to see that the greater scope for market forces within US HE compared with the UK and even more so elsewhere in Europe means that the worst features of US HE are any more extensive or egregious than those to be found in Government controlled systems, while, clearly, the very best of US HE eclipses the top end of HEIs in all other systems. The 'great debate' over the 2003 White Paper (brilliantly described and analysed in Robert Stevens (2004) *University to Uni: The politics of higher education in England since 1944*, London: Politico's/Methuen) and the 2004 Higher Education Bill is, when not to do with 'hidden agendas' over Blair v. Brown and the leadership of the Labour Party, really, like the recent furore about 'foundation hospitals', about whether HE is controlled by the State or (to some degree or other) left to the market. As William Rees-Mogg comments (*Times*, 12/1/04): the row over variable fees is the broader issue of 'the fallacy of the State...The difficulty is that decisions of the greatest importance are made on the limited information that can be processed by ministers...Ministers do not know what they are doing, of what the outcomes will be. When the Labour rebels say that there is no place for the market in higher education, they are saying that decisions should be taken solely by ministers, on limited and unreliable information.'

Stevens explores HE policy and sums it up as 'muddling through' over the decades:

- the universities are neglected, nationalised and debased while the MPs fight yesterday's battles ('The English (and I include for this purpose the Scottish) politicians on class are tiresome in the extreme.', and he quotes the *Economist* (25/1/03): 'the universities, especially those with any claim to elite status, turn the Chancellor [Brown] into a raving Jacobin');
- a political problem compounded by MPs selecting the wrong issue over which to man the class barricades (Stevens quotes Lord Desai, an academic economist Labour peer, 'For 35 years I have heard the

same argument: if we charge anything, the poor will not get access. The middle classes are clever; they always use the poor to justify their own subsidies...What is happening now is that by charging a single price we have to ration. Such rationing results in bad education...Who gets such bad education? People from lower income classes and ethnic minorities. They go to the ghastly universities.', and notes a photograph published in the *Daily Telegraph* (5/12/02) 'of an upper-class young woman carrying a placard' at a top-up fees protest which says it all, 'Save My Daddy's Money'!);

- a depressing national mess which, says Stevens, should 'remind one of Milton Friedman's warnings that when one starts tampering with the market, one has to go on tampering at an exponential rate' (or, indeed, one may recall the strictures of Adam Smith in Book IV, Chapter IX, *The Wealth of Nations*, on the necessity of limiting the role of the State given that it will, when trying to substitute for the free working of the market, 'always be exposed to innumerable delusions' and also given that when interfering in such complexity 'no human wisdom or knowledge could ever be sufficient'); and

- there being only one careful, objective and intellectually rigorous contribution to the debate, in the form of the 2003 Report of the Select Committee on Education and Skills, which 'actually thought about the long-term future of higher education' and duly proposed variable fees of up to £5000, but, of course, 'in the febrile atmosphere in which English politics is played out' this sensible, unanimous, all-party, 'remarkable achievement' of a Report has sunk without trace.

So, we have a Bill which proposes, by allowing variable annual tuition fees of up to £3K, to semi-deregulate HE as the last of the nationalised industries, but which is bitterly opposed and to those opponents Ministers stress that HE will still be a highly regulated market with its 'price' for UK citizens fixed by Government, along with the quantity of student places available as 'the product', and indeed increasingly also the Government will decide (via its HE Access Regulator) to which students as 'customers' these places may be 'sold'. One suspects Adam Smith would not approve of such modern bureaucratic interference, although he was by no means a fan in more laissez-faire times of eighteenth-century Oxford University's producer-oriented approach to its student-customers in the fulfilment of its duties under the contract to educate, complaining in a letter to a relative of 'the extraordinary and most extravagant fees we are obliged to pay the College and University on our admittance; it will be his own fault if anyone should endanger his health at Oxford by excessive study, our only business here being to go to prayers twice a day, and to lectures twice a week...'.

In Book V of *The Wealth of Nations* he is scathing about the Oxford Dons: 'In the University of Oxford, the greater part of the publick professors have, for these many years, given up altogether even the pretence of teaching...The discipline of colleges and universities is in general contrived, not for the benefit of the students, but for the interest, or more properly speaking, for the ease of the masters.' He would probably recognise that the equivalent risk nowadays is of poorly-funded and lowly-esteemed teaching being short-changed in the pursuit of less inadequately financed and much more career-enhancing research. It is also interesting to contemplate what Smith would make of the US 'trophy' professor, highly paid and largely an absentee from the campus where his/her teaching load is light or non-existent. Smith's solution to this market imperfection (whether in the Oxford of two hundred and fifty years ago, in the modern UK HE system, or in the any US Ivy League institution today) is the creation of what now we would label the empowered student-consumer: the payment of part of the tuition fees direct to the lecturer in return for 'deserving them, that is, by the abilities and diligence with which he discharges every part of his duty' rather than leaving him fully rewarded by a fixed, set salary even if he has performed his duty in 'as careless and slovenly a manner' as he can get away with.

If we substitute for Smith's part payment of fees direct to the academic with the payment of significant and variable tuition fees by the thereby newly empowered student-consumer direct to the modern HEI, and reduce the relative importance to the HEI of HEFCE 'T' block-grant as the modern equal to the fixed salary received by Smith's insufficiently motivated eighteenth century lecturer, we could claim Adam Smith as a likely supporter of the proposed variable tuition fees in the Higher Education Bill 2004, even if, at £3K, he would probably suspect the market will still not work efficiently in favour of either HEIs or their students. The answer is to remove the cap and for Oxford (see Appendix 3), and for others, to match Harvard's latest initiative (*New York Times* 29/2/04) in not charging fees at all to low-income families (up to $40k pa), and very little in fees to the next band (up to $60k). Such is, quite rightly, the social equity duty of the universities in helping low-income, high-ability students; it is a much wider task for Government, Society and pioneering charities such as the Sutton Trust, with, of course, the assistance of the universities, to help lower-acheiving, low-income students to qualify academically for, and aspire to, the best universities.

Overall, and looking out to 2025, if we think in terms of three models for the delivery of HE being the US mixed-economy public-private mass system, the continental European free public service mass systems, and the UK elite-in-style/mass-in-structure highly Government regulated but theoretically autonomous system, then the issue is whether: the US model will be challenged by the imposition of price-controls on its private sector and calls for greater accountability for/regulation of its public element, leaving the US moving slightly towards the UK model; the UK meanwhile will shift West and move towards the US model as it increases tuition fees and toys with marketisation; while the major European countries (France, Germany, Italy) will move slowly and painfully across the Channel as they too introduce meaningful tuition fees as a way of sharing the financial burden between taxpayer and student/family. Given that Australia, New Zealand and Canada have also already moved, via higher and variable tuition fees, towards the US model, one may well predict that globalisation in HE will mean a steady standardisation along the lines of the US HE system: mass (if not universal), diverse, an increasing presence for private (if not blatantly commercial) HEIs, students/families paying a greater part of the cost of HE via tuition fees which will vary amongst HEIs (and, unlike in the USA, perhaps also will vary across subjects within the HEI).

A few small and wealthy countries (Sweden, Norway, Denmark) with very strong social democratic traditions may resist such globalisation and continue to supply mass HE as a free public good, but even they may be forced to open up their HE systems as protected industries if the WTO/GATS negotiations really do proceed towards the liberalisation of trade in services such as HE. Given the role of English as the global language of the media, of academe, of scientific research and of commerce it is difficult to see how such a process of inevitable globalisation could do anything other than disproportionately benefit HE in both the US and the UK, providing the UK Government can resist the temptation to micromanage UK HE and also assuming that UK HE can avoid suffocating harmonisation within the proposed EU Higher Education Area.

Appendix 1

CHUCK GOES TO COLLEGE
THE ODYSSEY OF AN AMERICAN FAMILY FUNDING A BACHELORS DEGREE

It is a Saturday morning in the Fall of Chuck's 3rd year of his 4 year High School education, and Chuck is annoyed. He is annoyed because he is sitting at a desk in the auditorium of his school instead of in front of his new Sony Playstation. In front of him is a sheaf of foolscap newsprint papers marked 'Preliminary Scholastic Aptitude Test'; he has done no preparation for this exam (as he will do for the Scholastic Aptitude Test which he will sit two or three times next Fall), and he has no intention of paying much attention to it. He is treating it so lightly because he has no idea just how important this test actually is; what he also does not realise, and were he to do so he might view the morning with less complacency, is that the immense odyssey which is the application process for a university education (and its funding) in America begins right there, right then, at the very moment when the Football coach (who had to be in that afternoon anyway so was lumbered with administering the PSAT) will say: 'Open your booklets and begin section one'.

Chuck has never heard of a National Merit Scholarship; his twin sister Charlotte knows a girl in the year above them who became a National Merit Scholar but not even the girl herself realizes the importance of this distinction. The scholarships are awarded based on the combined scores which students receive on the PSAT; no matter who you are, no matter where you go to High School (even if your last name is Getty or Carnegie and you attend top private schools such as Choate or Deerfield), if your combined verbal and math scores are in the top-most fractions of percentages of the nation the Federal Government will pay part of the tuition costs of any university which you chose to attend. Furthermore, if you score particularly well (not even necessarily attaining an National Merit Scholarship) HE institutions both locally and nationally will begin to send you promotional material and you will already be deemed to be 'desirable' by those institutions, and by others, to which you may choose to apply—all of this will help you in your search for financial aid later in the process.

***

It is the late summer of Chuck and Charlotte's senior year in high school; the fall semester has just begun, but this time it is the turn of their father to be annoyed. He is filling out the dreaded Financial Aid Form or 'FAF'. It resembles nothing so much as a conductor's fold out score of an Opera for an entire orchestra; in it the father is asked to give every detail of his financial life and holdings: information on his Income Tax returns for one or more of the previous years, any savings he has, the value of any shares, any bonds, any real property and any automobiles. The author's head-master described filling in the form each and every year of a degree course as a labour of love. (Chuck's father believes it would be more aptly described as a labour of Hercules.) The Federal government will examine all the information provided by the father and assess what his eligibility for federal aid for each child will be. Based on the information provided to the Federal government, and probably by examining the federal figure (though procedures vary from state to state), the state in which the parent lives will also decide how much State Financial Aid (as opposed to Federal Financial Aid) each child 'needs'. Essentially if the father has any savings other than his pension, or if he and his wife have a combined income upwards of $40-50K per annum, he can expect to kiss them goodbye in the case of the former or to get well and truly stuck for an enormous bill in the case of the latter (which the student can offset by taking out commercial 'student loans' from high street banks which will charge below market, but still not entirely insubstantial, rates of interest).

The problem is that most families having a combined income of over $50K per annum also have a combined income of less than $120K—which is about the threshold point where paying full whack becomes almost bearable for a family. If Chuck and Charlotte's father is a successful accountant with his own business netting about $220K pa, or even better if he is married to a Doctor or a Lawyer who also makes a substantial income, then there is simply no problem—the family writes a cheque to the HEI (or perhaps pays on a credit card and earns many air-miles!). If Chuck and Charlotte's father is a successful middle-manager in either a service or manufacturing industry making around $65K pa, and even if he is married to a career-oriented wife who draws a salary of, say, $35K making a combined income of $100K, paying for the university education of the three children (or even two or one) will be a real stretch. The problem lies in the family being assessed as belonging to the 'upper middle income' and then assessed as able to pay the full whack. It is a sad fact of American HE that the bottom half of the middle-class is financially eviscerated by the cost of HE, while the upper half is substantially less affected: the 'affordability' debate discussed in the main body of this Paper.

Any aid which the three children might receive will come in a combination of four basic forms: 1) Federal, or State, Financial Aid: either in the form of outright grants (such as the famous Pell Grant) or in other forms of Federal aid covered under the so-called heading of 'Title IV'(of which the Pell Grant is a part). Title IV will give loans subsidised by the Government to be repaid at a substandard rate of interest and at a more lengthy overall schedule of repayment—but Title IV rarely if ever comes anywhere close to covering the entire cost of a university education. Likewise most states have parallel systems of aid which can be used at HEIs in the state—interestingly often private as well as public. Some states now operate state-wide scholarships akin to the National Merit Scholarships—Georgia's HOPE Scholarship Program being the prime example. 2) In the form of privately funded 'Student Loans' from commercial banks (High Street banks in UK jargon) which will be at a higher rate of interest than the Title IV loans, but a rate still lower than the average rate of interest for a loan; these will also likely have a more aggressive schedule of repayment. 3) Scholarships issued by the HEI itself; all HEIs (including state institutions) have part of the General Operating Budget for the year earmarked for 'tuition write-offs' in the form of internal scholarships. In the case of small private institutions the percentage of the Budget which is devoted to write offs can be very large (circa 40% to 60%); in the case of larger private or state institutions the percentage is smaller but it still substantial. 4) Need-based aid issued by the HEI itself; this will take either the form of specific endowments from alumni or corporations written in such a manner that the money cannot be used for anything else other than creating scholarships based on financial need rather than intellectual ability, or the form of a 'work study' job within the HEI.

'Work Study' is a simple plan: by keeping a substantial number of jobs within the HEI (generally work in Catering, Labs, the Student Union, the Library, etc.), structured in a form which allows three or four persons working below half-time to fill one full-time position, the HEI is able to employ students to fill these positions. This serves two purposes: first, it cuts the overall operating budget of the HEI by avoiding the benefits package which would be required to fill each of these full-time positions, and allows the positions to be filled only when needed during full semester/term operation (allowing the HEI to scale them down during Summer School operation or Vacation without laying off any workers);

second, it allows students to work for real wages within the University itself. Thus, those students are paid money (which their parents don't have to give them to spend since the parents are using said money to pay the tuition) for labour which is necessary, and that money can be used either to buy textbooks or to buy beer as the student's financial circumstances and general priorities dictate.

In general most students receive some Federal, some State, some Private and some Internal Financial Aid. The packages can be intricate or simple (an example of a simple package would be a student who has not won any merit based scholarships, and whose family is assessed as being ineligible for need-based aid, yet cannot come up with 100% of the fees up-front; in this case the student will simply take private loans to make up what his or her family cannot pay). At every HEI in America there is an 'Office of Financial Aid', and the persons employed in this office exist entirely to arrange aid packages to enable students to attend the HEI. Those persons will help the student by applying for available Federal and State Financial Aid and arranging and 'imprimaturing' applications for private loans—essentially speeding the process of assessment by the private lenders. The overall package of financial aid will depend upon a combination of the parent's financial circumstances and the raw intelligence of the child.

In practice, if the parents are *'affluent'* (or rather adjudicated so to be), the only way which Chuck or Charlotte will get financial aid is through a merit-based scholarship—which is not entirely unlikely since the children of middle-class and affluent families tend to be better educated (either as a result of being schooled in the private sector or, because funding for secondary state education is raised locally in America rather than centrally and then distributed state-wide, they will have benefited from living in wealthier neighbourhoods that have better funded schools). At the Federal level the only financial aid (other than loans) available for affluent families is through a National Merit Scholarship. At the state level they may be entitled to scholarship aid such as Georgia's HOPE Scholarship (if such a statewide system of merit scholarships exists in the given state) and most, though not necessarily all, HEIs have named endowments providing scholarships for young persons of exceptional intelligence. (Such scholarships allow nearly the full cost of the education to be met and those who both win them—thus abrogating the need to pay tuition—and can demonstrate a financial need—see below—will in practice receive enough financial aid to cover the room and board fees: thus they will get a 'free ride'). In Chuck and Charlotte's case the scholarship would cover the tuition and the family will be able to cover the room and board out of annual income.

If the family has a *median household income* (say between $25K and $50K), then they will be eligible for need-based financial aid in both grant and loan form at all three levels (Federal Financial Aid, State Financial Aid and specific Institutional Financial Aid from the HEI itself). If the child's raw intelligence is very high, he or she will be able to win the merit scholarships described above and obtain the 'free ride'. If the child does not have a high raw intelligence, he or she falls into the demographic niche which probably has the most difficulty funding an undergraduate degree in America. Clearly the student, or the family, will have to take loans from the private sector to cover the remainder of the cost of the education; it is probably persons from this background (and it is a substantial portion of the population) who build up the most debt in student loans stemming from their undergraduate education: it is on behalf of this not politically insignificant group that Congress gets agitated as tuition fees are hiked year on year.

If the family has a *low household income*, the student will get a substantial amount of Federal Financial Aid, State Financial Aid and Institutional Financial Aid in the form of need-based funding. If the child is of high raw intelligence, then he will be able to win enough merit scholarships (and in this case the need demonstrated has been substantial enough that the scholarships won will not necessarily have to be the 'flagship' merit scholarships described above—which they still might be—to make up the difference between the cost and need-based allowance; they may be a group of smaller scholarships: this is an example of a complicated package). If the child is not of high raw intelligence, then the difference between the need-based allowance, or the 'package' offered by the institution and the total cost, can usually be met with minimal loans from the private sector (this is especially true of a state HEI rather than a private— and students who fit into the 'low income, average raw intelligence' profile tend to enrol in state institutions), or by income earned by the student during and out of semester. Persons from this background tend, and I emphasize 'tend' as I am aware this is a generalization, to have a strong 'American work ethic' and see it as natural to work a substantial number of hours per week in addition to University coursework. (Whether, in fact, these grant/loan packages are keeping pace with 'the cost of college' is the 'access' debate discussed in the main body of this Paper.)

***

It is October in the Fall of Chuck and Charlotte's senior (final) year in High School. They are spending part of the evenings this week preparing for the SAT (Scholastic Aptitude Test) which they will take on the morning of Saturday. Though the test is administered by a private body and has no governmental connections whatsoever, it is essentially mandatory; virtually every HEI in America uses it to assess students, and declining to sit the SAT will be a substantial disadvantage even if students choose to apply only to institutions which do not require it (see below). Theoretically the test 'does exactly what it says on the label'— tests the aptitude, or raw intelligence, of students in both verbal and numerical areas. The test is a multiple-choice format with an answer sheet which must be filled in using a #2 pencil, has a 'verbal' and a 'mathematical' section (each of which has subdivisions) and takes three hours to sit overall—the various sub-sections are each administered under different time protocols. The answers are marked electronically; there is no opportunity for extemporary response (other than in a recently introduced essay section). The test does not seek to ascertain what the student has learned in secondary education, but rather his or her capacity to learn at the tertiary level. As such the test does not ask specific factual questions (in the verbal section) but rather asks the student, for instance, to analyse the linguistic relationship between pairs of words and choose one of four pairs that is most similarly related to a given example.

The purpose of the test is to attempt to create a level playing field for students to compete upon: it is supposed to cancel out any difference in the quality of the teaching or resources which a more well-funded school may have provided. There are various sections of the Verbal section of the SAT each of which seeks to use a different psychometric evaluation to gain an overall picture of the student's raw intelligence. Likewise the numerical sections of the test attempt primarily to ascertain the problem solving skills of the student rather than outright mathematical knowledge. Though it is fairly well acknowledged that the SAT has internal flaws (as all psychometric testing does) the importance of SAT scores cannot be underestimated. Fair or not, the primary factors involved in the initial step in evaluation of the applicant by the Admissions Office of a given HEI will be: 1) the high school GPA; and 2) the SAT scores. If the former is extremely high and the second mediocre, the conclusion is likely to be that the school's standards were too undemanding to give an accurate picture of the student's ability. Only very rarely is the mirror image of this paradigm true, i.e. the student's SAT scores are very high and the grades are very low; students who score well on the SAT come from backgrounds where school performance is valued. Recommendations and submitted writing samples (usually in the form of 'entrance essays' come a distant third, and are only taken into account after the student has passed the initial assessment and his file has been passed onto the admissions committee for that year).

The Scholastic Aptitude Test is administered seven times a year: in October, November, December, January, March, May, and June; always on a Saturday morning. Students may take the test as many times as they wish, though most universities average the scores. Because of this it is arguable whether it is in a student's advantage to take the test several times; if the student scores highly the first time it is probably not, though if he scores below what he believes himself capable of he probably should—the danger is that he may score lower, pulling down his aggregate score. There now exists a facility to cancel, or erase from the records a given score from a given Saturday, by contacting the testing body (Educational Testing Services) within five days of sitting the exam, long before the test is marked or the mark reported, so, if a student feels that he or she has substantially under performed through illness or other factors, he or she may erase that performance from the records. ETS will automatically report the scores of the test to four HEIs chosen by the student as a part of the package provided by the registration fee, and to as many others as the student requests for additional fees.

The current charge is $26.00 for the SAT (including reporting to four HEIs) and $6.50 for reporting the score to each additional HEI. Since most students apply to more than four institutions (even if they are intending to apply in-state), and probably to about an average of six to eight, the registration fee for each and every time a given student takes it is likely to be between $35.00 and $50.00. There is also the opportunity, for additional fees, to take 'subject tests' which last one hour each and are available on the afternoons of the Saturdays. The subject tests are designed to test what a student has learned in his high school class. The basic subjects offered are Math, Biology, Languages, Listening and Writing (the writing test is the only opportunity within the SAT to give an extemporaneous answer). These tests are not weighted as heavily by admissions offices as the general tests are, and only serve to provide an opportunity for students to distinguish themselves against their peers; in other words they operate by reinforcing the grades already earned in a class—a university is more likely to believe that an 'A-' earned in a Biology class in a large state high school situated in a less than prosperous area is actually worth an 'A-' if the student takes the SAT subject test and scores well in it.

ETS effectively has no competition. There is a second national testing board called the ACT, but it is not anywhere near as powerful.

91

Traditionally tied to the region of the southern states of America the ACT is designed to create a national testing system which assesses the actual knowledge of the student. For some years many institutions, and especially the Northern Ivy League institutions, would not even look at the ACT. This has changed, but not dramatically. The ACT website (www.act.org) now claims that: 'The ACT Assessment tests are universally accepted for college admission. The ACT Assessment is now accepted by virtually all colleges and universities in the U.S., including all of the Ivy League schools' (but the test is simply not in any way as influential as the SAT). The website further claims that: 'The ACT Assessment is not an aptitude or an IQ test. Instead, the questions on the ACT are directly related to what you have learned in your high school courses in English, mathematics, and science. Because the ACT tests are based on what is taught in the high school curriculum, students are generally more comfortable with the ACT than they are with the traditional aptitude tests or tests with narrower content'. Having said all of this, if a student applies to an institution having taken the ACT and not the SAT, the institution will wonder why (and probably conclude that the student was attempting to avoid a poor performance on the SAT). Furthermore, precisely because the ACT is subject based, schools can structure their curriculum according to what the ACT expects students to know; in other words it is much easier for a school to 'teach to the test' (by reading old examinations) for the ACT than the SAT (although, to a degree, this too can be taught to/prepared for). Interestingly the fees are almost identical for both tests and it will shock no one that the number of institutions which the basic fee covers reporting the score to is four (ACT only charges a basic fee of $25.00—a savings of one dollar—but charges $7.00 per extra score reported—an extra two dollars if the posited average of eight institutions is taken as an example; making it effectively one dollar more expensive, or in fact exactly equal if the scores are sent to six institutions). The charges are so similar that one wonders why the cartel regulators have not become involved.

***

It is the late Fall through Winter of Chuck and Charlotte's senior year: the period of mid-November through about 15 February; they are using this time to fill out about eight separate application to eight different institutions. Each form is individual to the institution, even the ones for separate state institutions in the same state. This effectively means that the same information must be produced on eight separate forms (contrast the much more stream-lined UCAS procedure in the UK). Though having said that, the term 'repetition' is not precisely true, because each form will have a differently phrased set of questions which allows the applicant the opportunity to present the information in a way which fits the ethos of the given HEI, and this is an important part of the application process in America—especially in the private sector. Indeed, the applicant verges on the supplicant in being expected by some 'top colleges' to display 'demonstrated interest' in the given HEI, even to the extent of showering its Admissions Office with e-mails to convince HEI X that he/she really wants to be accepted above all at X even if applications have been made also to A, B, C...K, L, M (of course, the canny applicant may well be sending such e-mails to all 15 HEIs!).

There was a move, beginning about a decade ago, to make some sort of common application used by a majority of US HEIs, and indeed a small (but not completely insignificant) portion of the private sector recognised the 'Common App.'. The project never really caught on, however, and today only around 230 HEIs accept or suggest using the application. There was and is, however, still a distinct advantage in using the HEI's own application form because it demonstrates a form of commitment to the HEI in question. By taking the time to fill in the institution's own form one demonstrates a genuine desire to attend that institution (i.e. it shows that the application was not merely one of an enormous range made using copies of the Common App. in a 'shotgun' approach to college admissions—in other words if you fire off enough applications at once one of them is bound to score a hit; Common App. is the most efficient way of implementing the shotgun approach to application). Whether or not admissions committees do it consciously, and to be fair they probably do not, there is (though probably not a pre-judiciam against Common App. candidates) an un-quantifiable 'benefit of the doubt' given to candidates who use the HEI's own form. The application process becomes ever-more formal, tactical, and scripted, and especially in respect of 'top colleges' (where also much time and effort is devoted by applicants and their driver-parents in touring the Ivies, and even in hiring a 'college application coach').

An additional deterrent to the shotgun approach to college application, is the application fees charged by each HEI, though once again the middle class and wealthy have an advantage here. The fees range from at least $40 up to well over $100 (making the well-resourced, professional admissions office at some popular HEIs almost self-financing, as yet another example of how far UK HEIs have to go if they are to close the funding gap with US HE). Though state institutions charge less, as a rule one can expect to pay a figure which will be equivalent to around $70-80 per application. Obviously the total will fluctuate from applicant to applicant depending principally upon the total number of institutions applied to and the percentage of those which are state institutions. But, taking Chuck and Charlotte as our 'Middle-America example', and taking the following reasonable assumptions about their applications: three are state institutions charging around $40-50, three are Liberal Arts colleges or private universities charging around $80, and two are premier institutions charging around $120, the total figure of $620 per child is arrived at. That means that their father is looking at a bill of $1,240, plus at least $200 per child for the SATs, which adds up to around $1,800 just for the application process alone (over £1000, or £500-plus for each child, compared with the UK UCAS fee of £10 each!).

None of these fees is avoidable; there is no financial aid available for any of them; there is no means-testing and no grants to pay for them if the family is not in a position to do so (although help may be available from churches, Rotary/Lions, and similar charities; and some 'top colleges' do invite poor applicants to seek a waiver of such fees). So, though for the posited 'Middle America' family the circa $900 per child is not a real deterrent, for a lower middle class or working class family it is and the child will probably apply to fewer institutions and a higher proportion of state institutions. This is ironic because the intelligent child of a low income family is the 'holy grail' searched for by admissions officers across the land, and would be aggressively recruited through generous financial aid packages and work-study jobs, were the family able to come up with the application fees to enable the candidate to appear on the given HEI's radar screen in the first place. A circumstance which, to be fair, is not impossible, or even unfeasible, because candidates in this circumstance foresee its arising and take steps to avoid it: often by saving up money from a summer job in their junior year of High School or by working part-time in the evenings of their senior year—most American High School students, even those with a wealthy background, have a part-time job of some sort due to the American work ethic. None of this, though, changes the fact that those who have the least financial advantages must work harder to become noticed regardless of intellect: which is disturbing—but inevitable within the operating system.

**

It is any time from the fall through the spring of Chuck and Charlotte's senior year in High School; they are visiting universities and colleges which they have an interest in and wish to assess the atmosphere of. They may do this before applying in order to judge whether the institution will be right for them and they for the institution, or they may visit after an offer has been made by the college. While there they will sleep on the floor of student rooms belonging to volunteers participating in the 'recruitment' process, be plied with enormous amounts of illegal alcohol (presuming the campus is not 'dry') and other forms of entertainment by various Fraternities and Sororities, meet the friends of their 'host' students, eat in the dining halls, sit in on a couple of classes, and generally attempt to participate in the life of the institution over a day or two—or even three.

This is a time when the choice of where the student wishes to receive his or her tertiary education is made; Chuck and Charlotte have already applied to these institutions (or if it is the fall will already be considering applying to these institutions) so the academic reputation of the institutions is not really a factor—though it is possible their parents will allow them to visit a few institutions in the fall which they would never conceive of allowing their children to attend simply because the child shows an interest and the parents do not wish to quash the interest at that point for fear of quashing interest in visiting universities and colleges generally. The visits are a very important time for the perspective students because they will allow a student to obtain a realistic 'feel' for the institution: whether it is too large (or too small), whether it is too socially orientated (i.e. too many parties over the weekend) or too orientated towards the academic side of 'College Life' at the expense of social activity and the opportunity to grow socially over the formative years of 18-21, whether there is a balanced mixture of male and female students, whether the curriculum is too orientated towards lecturing and testing, or whether it is too orientated towards continual written assessment in the form of each class (of the four or five per semester the student will take) requiring two or three 'papers' to be written.

Some combination of these factors: academic structure, social structure, assessment paradigms, religious ethos (if any), social ethos, pastoral ethos of the institution, etc, will appeal to the student. Usually he or she will come away with two or three institutions where he or she believes that he or she would be happy. Remarkably, in the instances where the student feels that he or she would only be happy in one institution, provided that the student does not have an exaggerated opinion of his or her own abilities, than the ethos will match so well that the student will usually be accepted there—this is most often the case when a student fixes his or her heart on a particular Liberal Arts College. If the student is visiting in the fall he or she will apply to these institutions along with several second choice institutions; if he or she is visiting in the spring he or she will return to the family dinner table to discuss the choice with family and to await the offers of financial aid. Early applications may be crucial in the case of 'top colleges' which are highly selective: Princeton, for example, admits only 10% or so of all applicants, and half of the entry is chosen from such early applicants.

***

Which brings us to the final stage in the process: the offers. Chuck and Charlotte will receive financial aid offers after their acceptance. These will vary in size depending upon how much the institution wants to have Chuck or Charlotte as a student.

Realistically each of them will be presented with three or four 'live options' for attendance. It then becomes a family choice of deciding on what represents the best value for money. If Charlotte has her heart set on Smith and the offer she receives from Smith is $4,000 more expensive than her offer from Vasser, and $2,500 less than her offer from Boden (all good private institutions with similar teaching methodologies and social struc-tures—though Smith is still a women's college it is part of a group of col-leges situated close to one another and there are 'men everywhere'), it becomes a choice of whether the extra $6,500 is worth it. If Boden is her third choice and money is an issue she will probably go to Boden regard-less. If money is not an issue she will go to Smith. If the case is really bor-derline and Vasser is her sixth choice while Smith is still first, she might have to go to Vasser—I say 'might' because families choosing between institutions of this genre do make a real effort to send the child to the institution he or she most wants to attend. (Because of this figures in the region of $2,500 p.a. rarely are a determining factor, though this still adds up to a minimum of $10,000 over four years; figures of $6,500 are definite-ly a factor because it is much more immediately clear that it will create a hefty extra $25,000 over four years). Looking at another genre of choice: if Chuck has a choice between Notre Dame, Georgetown, Creighton, and Fordham (all good Roman Catholic institutions) but is determined to attend an urban campus, then it comes down to whether his parents are willing to pay the extra money (and it will undoubtedly be more) for Georgetown rather than Fordham; if Chuck's family is wealthy and wants to follow his mother's example and go to Medical School, then the pres-tige of Georgetown is probably worth the extra money. In three years time if Charlemagne decides he wants to attend a large university, he will probably be looking at similar offers from several out-of-state flagship campuses and an offer from one or more in-state institutions; if he lives in the South and is clever the offers will probably be UVA (presuming he lives in Virginia; if he does not he will have to be very clever indeed to be admitted out-of-State), UNC, UT Knoxville, Maryland, and possibly USC Charleston. Two of the four have better reputations than the others, UVA and UNC in that order, and will be worth the already lower fees than his siblings will be paying for their private institutions. (Charlemagne's father was seen dancing around the back yard screaming 'Hallelujah!' after his third child announced that a large State institution was the sort of institution he wished to attend.)

In the end, if money is not an issue, the child will attend one of the top three choices where he is accepted; the offers will not necessarily be near identical from one institution to another, and a specific sort of financial aid which the child qualifies for might exist at one of those institutions. If money is an issue, the child will be sent where the offer is best—either that or he or she will incur enormous loans and the family will suffer major austerity for several years. If money is an enormous issue—i.e. the family is destitute and the child is not intelligent—then the realistic option will be the community college system where the child can work full-time, attend classes part-time, and earn credits at his or her own pace—and perhaps transfer to a 4-year state institution near him or her later where he or she will be able to continue part-time study and full-time work.

The 'bidding wars' which have made large press in the past are, in reality, rare. When an HEI makes an offer it has done quite a lot of actuarial modelling to arrive at it. It most likely knows what the family can afford and will make the offer at the absolute maximum it believes it can get. The stories about families trying to squeeze an extra three thousand dollars out of one institution by using the offer of another institution are misleading. Families will attempt to 'bargain' but they will rarely get more than $1,000-1,500 out of the negotiations—and unless the family is poor that sort of figure will not make a substantial difference in whether or not the child attends a given institution. This is becoming more and more true; during the mid 1980s bargaining was rampant. But through the course of the period of about 1988 onwards HEIs stopped practicing policies of so called 'need-blind' admission. When faced with four or five students with equivalent GPAs, SATs, recommendations and written work: they simply began to give the offer to the student who was assessed as able to pay (although a bright, poor/minority background applicant will probably be showered with offers of financial aid if he/she has the necessary high entry grades for a wealthy private HEI).

But, whatever the circumstances, whatever the choice of institution, whatever the projected debt, and whatever the costs, it remains a fact that America has a higher percentage of participation in higher education, though admittedly a lower level of completion, than the UK and most, if not all, of its OECD partners. Eventually Chuck, Charlotte and Charlemagne will bundle their clothes, stereo, a few books (and usually a television and video game system) into the family estate wagon (be it a 2003 Volvo or a 1978 Chevrolet) and be driven off to college: where there will be tearful goodbyes with parents and the new Odyssey which is the four years of a Liberal Arts education will begin.

Dr Luke Wright, Research Officer, OxCHEPS

Appendix 2

PRICING THE PRODUCT
MANIC MARKETPLACE OR COSY CARTEL?

So, amidst much anger and angst, New Labour proposes top-up tuition fees of up to £3K p.a. from after the next General Election and hence for application in 2006/07 (and then not to be increased, other than by RPI, until after the following General Election in c2011). This Appendix attempts to explore what factors will influence a university in deciding the level of fee (if any) to charge within the upper limit and whether to charge differentially across its range of degree courses (say, law, management and medicine, compared with philosophy, theology and nursing). These factors primarily include: the economic theory of pricing and deciding what-the-market-will-really-bear, presumably risking bankruptcy if a university prices itself out of the market or a local crisis if it overprices its law, physics, or golf studies degree; and the legal context in terms of competition law and avoiding a prison sentence for the VC who is found guilty of engaging in a cosy cartel with his/her mates at a supposedly competitor university...

Clearly, the analogue for the proposed Brave New World of a (partially) de-regulated and (partly) marketised UK HE industry is the US mixed-economy public/private HE system and the fees charged in its private 'not-for-profit' universities and colleges (and also at its growing number of 'for-profit' HEIs): see chapters 2 and 3. While the British fumble towards £3K p.a. max for each year of the average three year degree course, the typical public US State university annual tuition fee for the standard four (and often in practice nearly five) year Liberal Arts undergraduate degree is already above £3K and with some States talking of big increases (over 40% in New York State; 10% + in California). The private university fees range from £10K to £25K, and any out-of-State student at a State university will also be paying around £10K p.a. (i.e. like the 'economic cost' fee applied to non-UK/EU students in UK HE). What is the experience of the US private universities in themselves setting these prices (as opposed to a few of the State institutions having the fee set for them by the politicians)?

First, consider the application of US federal anti-trust laws (the

Sherman Act and the Clayton Act) to HE. The universities are no longer treated as non-commercial exceptions: as the judge commented in *United States v Brown University* (805 f. Supp. 288, E.D. Pa. 1992), '... The court can conceive of few aspects of higher education more commercial than the price charged to students' (at 289). (See Kaplin, W.A. & Lee, B.A. (1995) *The Law of Higher Education*, pp 762-768; and Richmond, D., 'Private College and Tuition Price-Fixing: an Anti-trust Primer', 17 J. Coll. & Univ.Law 271, 1991.) It needs to be noted (with concern by VCs!) that the stringent US anti-trust laws are the model for recent UK legislation in the form of the Competition Act 1998 and the Enterprise Act 2002. Competition law covers the territory once known as 'monopolies and mergers', such as anti-competitive practices, restrictive trade practices, and abuses of a dominant market position/power; the OFT, and even the EU Commission (under Articles 81 & 82 of the European Treaty), can seek hefty penalties. Defining 'dominant' and 'market' is, of course, fees and fun for the lawyers: the key question would be whether the HEIs concerned are effectively a 'substantial' part of the 'relevant' market. Now define 'substantial' and 'relevant'; the former is 25%-40%, and the latter depends on whether the degree can in practice recruit nationally or just locally. Note that franchising deals may need special care... Also note that the Education Secretary is already on to the perceived risk of at least some VCs forming a cosy cartel! The *Financial Times* (26/2/03, p6) carried the headline: 'Universities warned over creation of fees cartel'. When asked whether Russell Group VCs exhibited aspects of cartel-like behaviour, Charles Clarke is quoted as saying: 'You might say that - I couldn't possibly comment.'. The OFT has echoed the warning (*Times Higher*, 7/3/03). And the OFT has, under the Competition Act 1998, fined Argos £17m and Littlewoods £5m over price-fixing in relation to board games! It is also currently investigating alleged 'fee-fixing' amongst independent schools. VCs, therefore, need to note with care that the Enterprise Act 2002 allows for prison sentences of up to 5 years; similar US antitrust legislation already despatches around 30 executives to gaol each year...

For further analysis see Chapter 28 of Palfreyman, D. & Warner, D. (2002) *Higher Education Law*; Furse, M. (2002) *Competition Law of the UK and EC*; and Frazer, T. et al (2003) *Enterprise Act 2002: The New Law of Mergers, Monopolies and Cartels*. Frazer, et al, refer to 'the draconian cartel offence'! This 'criminalisation' of competition law creates a new 'cartel offence' and involves strong criminal sanctions (five years in prison and/or an unlimited fine), and provides extensive powers of investigation for the OFT (including covert and intrusive surveillance). There are also new rights for civil claims for damages where a customer or competitor has suffered financial losses as a result of price-fixing. The cartel offence in s188(1) arises where an individual 'dishonestly agrees with one or more other persons to make or implement, or to cause to be made or implemented, arrangements relating to at least two undertakings'; 'undertakings' includes HEIs, and 'arrangements' are described in s188(2) as price-fixing, limiting supply, market-sharing, customer-sharing, bid-rigging...The test for dishonesty is whether the individual's actions were dishonest by the ordinary standards of reasonable and honest people and whether the defendant realised his actions were dishonest (*R v Ghosh* [1982] QB 1053, CA). The OFT can give immunity to anybody (other than an instigator or leader within the cartel) involved in and then whistle-blowing on cartel activities (s190(4)): as Frazer notes, 'These sanctuary provisions are extraordinary'.

Second, in setting degree prices, the US institutions always charge the same for any undergraduate degree, whether the student has majored in 'expensive' laboratory-based Physics (although an annual modest $100-150 'lab fee' may be charged) or in 'cheap' classroom-based English Literature (and remember that Law and Management are usually taught as very expensive Graduate School courses, alongside Medicine). But how do they decide whether they are a $15K 'school' or a $25K one? Crudely, they charge what-the-market-will-bear ('value-based pricing' rather than 'cost-oriented pricing'), and that depends on their reputation/brand image; it may also link to what other similar HEIs charge ('competitor-oriented pricing'), providing it does so only loosely and is not a price-fixing cartel! (Bearing in mind, of course, that often the high 'sticker-price' is paid only by a minority of students; many get a discount by way of a bursary and/or get offered financial aid by way of cheap loans and campus jobs; and also bearing in mind that one observer sees 'ominous implications' for most US private HEIs as the 1990s boom ends, along with a golden age for steadily pushing up fees - as similarly have UK independent schools at double or treble RPI each year: Geiger, R.L. (2000), 'Politics, Markets, and University Costs', CSHE Research and Occasional Papers at ishi.lib.berkeley.edu/cshe.) See also chapters 4 and 5.

The most accessible exploration of the funding of US HE is Ehrenberg, R.G. (2000) *Tuition Rising: Why College Costs So Much* (see also his useful web-site at ipr.cornell.edu/rgespage/ronshome). He stresses that US HEIs are weak at holding down their costs - they find it difficult to say No; also they are in an arms-race to improve campus facilities, to recruit and retain the best faculty, to pursue research... and, at a time of economic boom, they have had to face little consumer resistance. There is also Middaugh, M.F. (2000) *Analysing Costs in Higher Education* ('New

Directions for Institutional Research', No. 106, Jossey-Bass Publishers): for detail, see † below, and refer back to chapter 2.

The top 25/30 'élite' UK universities can easily get away with charging the maximum allowed £3K tuition fee from 2006/07 given that they have the reputation/brand image to demand in effect exactly what-the-market-will-(or in fact must)bear (and can probably do so without falling foul of the OFT's enforcement of anti-competition legislation, since, with only a little creative accounting, they can show that their costs of providing the degrees anyway exceed the price). The bottom 20/30 may be able to risk only a few 'star' courses being charged at the full £3K pa, or even anywhere near it. In between there will (initially) be confusion as the market evolves: what can a 'posh-poly' get away with compared to a 3rd decile 'old' university (Oxford Brookes, Brighton, Bournemouth v Keele, Hull, Bradford)? Dare OB go for £3K across-the-board, or only for Law, Town Planning and Management? Will Keele discount heavily on Philosophy, Sociology and Education? How will Hull fare? - 'Oop North' with cheap housing but not a disco capital à la Manchester and Leeds, and hovering on the edge of being 'teaching only'? (And, anyway, what's wrong with being 'teaching only'? Dartmouth College in the USA has very high fees and its undergraduates go on to become research students at Harvard, Yale, Princeton, Berkeley, etc., or take up strongly competed for and expensive graduate school places in Law, Medicine and Business at such prestigious universities... yet Dartmouth's academic staff are not required to be 'research active' and it does not award research degrees.)

Or must any self-respecting UK university charge the full £3K to avoid giving the impression that it's not 'top-notch', and will it then quietly discount (in the way that BA pretends all Business Class seats are full-price but, low and behold, you can save 25% via a middle-man selling you a sham mini-holiday with hotel B & B you won't be using)? Oh, and will you get air-miles and Nectar points if you pay the tuition fee up-front and in cash? Moreover, it would indeed be dangerous to 'cartel' a £2250 price for all 22 hospitality degree courses up and down the land, when the cost of delivering them just must vary from, say, Northumbria to UWE. Engineering, Physics and Chemistry, especially if 4-year courses, could easily price themselves out of the market if any of HEIs 30-60 get too ambitious: a price-war could result. On the other hand, enterprising HEIs may offer accelerated two-year degrees, allowing the student to save on a year of accommodation costs and a year of fees (perhaps then charging £3K for each of two years, when otherwise the HEI's brand image might suggest only £1500 pa over 3 years) – indeed, some HEIs may yet become properly customer-oriented!

So, what does the pricing textbook tell us? (Monroe, K.B. (2003), *Pricing*. McGraw-Hill.) Well, lessons one to four are: *Know Your Costs* (Do we in HE have a truly sophisticated and robust financial model of the HEI? - Not really, but OxCHEPS is working on one: see the reference to the NACUBO costing mechanism for US HEIs in chapter 3 and Appendix 3 on the costing Oxford project); *Know your Demand* (We may be about to find out the hard way when we up the fees that it is not as strong as we hoped! - Government says HEIs have real autonomy in (only) one area, freedom to go bust!); *Know Your Competition and Your Market* (Who will be first with the two year degree where five months of the year is not spent on holiday, and will others speedily follow, or will we be slow and leave the US 'for-profit' private distance-learning Phoenix University (and others) to move in under GATS?- as already noted, HEIs may yet become truly customer-oriented and ditch a teaching year based on medieval society's need for students to have a Summer Long Vacation in order to go home and help with the Harvest!); *Know Your Objectives* (Is the HEI ready to admit/boast it is 'a teaching only' university? And thereby making a marketing virtue of a financial necessity!).

So, get busy with that SWOT analysis, and start applying all the other tools and techniques to be found in, say, Kotler, P. (1995) *Strategic Marketing for [US] Educational Institutions*, and Kotler & Andreasen (2003) *Strategic Marketing for Non-Profit Organisations*, as well as in Chapman, D. & Cowdell. T. (1998) *New Public Sector Marketing*, or indeed in any general marketing textbook. See also Sargeant, A (1999) *Marketing Management for Non-Profit Organisations*. The essence of the Andreasen/Kotler message is a need for a customer-centred organisational mindset; and not only for creating new courses/improving student recruitment (pp 99-110 & 356-360), but also in terms of fundraising as discussed in chapter 7 (in 2001 4 of the US top 20 fundraising charities were universities - Stanford at $580m, in donations/legacies, Harvard at $485m, Duke at $408m, and Yale at $358m). Kotler (1995) is especially useful - see * below for detail... Sargeant covers fund-raising in Chapter 5, and education (including HE) in Chapter 7, all from a UK perspective. Finally, there is: Mike Boxall on marketing HE in *Universities in the Marketplace* (CUA/Touche Ross, 1991); and Gibbs, P. & Knapp, M. (2001) *Marketing Higher and Further Education*, along with Gibbs, P. (2002) 'From the invisible hand to the invisible hand-shake: marketing higher education' in Research in Post-Compulsory Education 7 (3) 325-337 - see ** below for more detail, and for further 'marketing HE' references...

And what about higher fees 'empowering' the student as an increasingly value-for-money aware consumer? The student: HEI 'contract to educate' is a consumer contract in the context of HE as a service industry (see Chapter 29 of Palfreyman, D. & Warner, D. (2002) *Higher Education Law*, as updated/supplemented on the OxCHEPS web-site at the 'Law Update' Page and at the 'Law Casebook' Page). Consumer law requires that the HEI teaches 'with reasonable care and skill' (s13 Supply of Goods and Services Act 1982); here 'reasonable means to the standard of the average HEI (just as the doctor, architect, engineer, solicitor is negligent if he/she falls below the standard of the reasonably competent member of his/her profession). The Unfair Contract Terms Act 1977 and, more significantly, the Unfair Terms in Consumer Contracts Regulations 1999 each also apply to restrict the HEI's use of 'small print' or 'get-out' clauses, importing the concept of 'good faith' and the scrutiny of the Office of Fair Trading. Finally, if a university engaged in really dodgy second-hand car dealer practices, the criminal sanctions of the Trade Descriptions Act 1968 might kick-in (as seen also with the package holiday industry as the perhaps nearest commercial equivalent to modern HE!). In addition, there is 'misrepresentation' within contract law: the HEI prospectus/course handbook promises what the staff/library can't deliver as marketing outpaces production; already two mature undergraduates have settled out-of-court in their favour against HEIs delivering allegedly under-resourced Law degrees, and a very recent County Court decision (*Rycotewood College*, February 2003: see Palfreyman in *Education and the Law* 16 (4), 2003; also see the OxCHEPS 'Law Update' ('New Material') and 'Law Case-book' Pages at oxcheps.new.ox.ac.uk) has given a number of aggrieved students general damages along with £2500 each for 'disappointment': thereby extending the severe limitations on awarding 'mental distress' damages in breach of contract cases beyond the usual spoilt-holiday/package tour cases - see *Higher Education Law*, Chapter 29 and the on-line update to para. 29.38 at the OxCHEPS web-site.

UK HE, therefore, is about to live in (even more) interesting times as it (select phrase according to political views!) [either partly escapes the dead-hand of Government/Quango over-regulation and micro-management][or sadly is crudely marketised, is pushed into a semi-commercial world and ceases to be fully public good/service]. It now needs in relation to its core product (the undergraduate degree) to discover the mystery of supply/demand and costing/pricing...Get ready for the training courses on 'Janet & John go marketing' and 'Noddy discovers costing & pricing'; the management consultants will, of course, be delighted (at a price!) to help you invent a pricing strategy, complete with sales, special offers, discounts, Nectar points - all the usual tactics except perhaps 'two degrees for the price of one'! (Of course, Oxford University still awards an MA along with the BA!).

† Middaugh (2000) – see also chapters 2 and 3:

a This collection of essays explores whether US private university costs are out of control (there is a similar debate in the USA in relation to health care): the 1998 National Commission on the Cost of Higher Education (NCCHE, Congress) reported on the 'veil of obscurity' clouding, and the 'financial opacity' of, HEI accounts. There is the threat of Government stepping in to reduce US HEI costs. It is recognised the 'the schemes used to allocate indirect costs [overheads] are, if not arbitrary, at least imprecise' (p.10) - a weakness which 'remains stubbornly true' despite great effort, given that much is often built on 'a heroic assumption'. Similarly, the allocation of capital costs is also 'a daunting task'. Moreover, since universities are non-profit operations, they tend to be 'revenue maximisers' but have little incentive to be 'cost minimisers' providing the former equals or very slightly exceeds the latter by increasing tuition fees year-on-year.

b One big problem is whether student financial aid is simply a price discount or rather a legitimate production cost, but a bigger fuzzy area is accounting for the cost of physical capital (land, buildings and equipment): 'The neglect of capital distorts calculated educational costs by 25 to 40 percent.' (p. 37). And the biggest fuzziness? - costs allocation across undergraduate teaching and postgraduate teaching and research.

c All this makes pricing the product on the basis of cost, rather than what-the-market-will-bear, rather problematic, even for US HEIs better used for longer to costing and pricing the product: as Winston puts it (p 99), 'Private sector: price = cost + profit, Higher Education: price = cost - subsidy.' That said, the proposed White Paper cap of £3K p.a. on tuition fees for English HEIs means that no HEI at £3K can cover its costs as properly calculated, and any lesser fee is clearly based not on being 'leaner and meaner' but reflects the HEI's expectation that the potential student-consumer will not value the HEI's degree products sufficiently to pay more than a certain figure.

* Kotler (1995) deals specifically with the marketing of education (schools, colleges and universities, in a US context):

a The key concepts are:
   • responsiveness to the customer-student.

- focus on customer-student satisfaction.
- enhance customer-student value (price-quality).
- create a quality-delivery system (including a complaints system).
- benchmark against other (good!) HEIs.
- apply the principles and techniques of market research, marketing strategy and planning, and market segmentation; along with the theory of consumer behaviour, product development, and pricing.

b On 'Pricing Educational Programmes' (Chapter 12, pp 306-328) the Kotler emphasis is on understanding how the student perceives price as the consumer, his/her personal cost-benefit analysis to determine the expected/hoped-for value of attending university X rather than university Y (note 'consumers seem wary of schools [universities] that charge significantly less than comparable schools', p 313; but also beware the existence for every university of 'a psychological price barrier', p 314).

** Gibbs (2002) is something of an antidote to Kotler. Gibbs argues for trust to be part of a marketing relationship between student and HEI, rather than the simplistic application of the principles of 'for profit' marketing reducing HE to a consumption good, bringing about the commodification and consumerisation of HE learning: he calls for 'a reconceptualised marketing mix' where the '4 Ps' (product, price, place, promotion) are replaced in an HE context by the '4 Cs' (concept, cost, channel, communication) in 'the learner relationship model of marketing' as 'a move away from Smith's invisible hand towards... the invisible handshake'. Gibbs credits the '4 Cs' and 'the invisible handshake' as below, and cites other useful material...

Berger, K.A. & Wallingford, H.P. (1996) Developing Advertising and Promotion Strategies for Higher Education, Journal of Marketing for Higher Education, 7(4) pp. 61-72.

Duncan, J.G. (1989) Marketing of Higher Education: problems and issues in theory and practice, Higher Education Quarterly, 43, pp. 175-188.

Jugenheimer, D.W. (1995) Advertising the University: a professional approach to promoting the college or university, Journal of Marketing for Higher Education, 6, pp. 1-22.

Koku, P.S. (1997) What is in a Name? The Impact of Strategic Name Change on Student Enrolment in Colleges and Universities, Journal of Marketing for Higher Education, 8(2), pp. 53-71.

Liu, S.S. (1998) Integrating Strategic Marketing on an Institutional Level, Journal of Marketing for Higher Education, 8(4), pp. 17-28.

Okun, A.M. (1980) The Invisible Handshake and the Inflationary Process, Challenge, 23, pp. 5-12.

Wasmer, D.J. Williams, J.R. & Stevenson, J. (1997) A Reconceptionalization of the Marketing Mix: using the 4 C's to Improve Marketing Planning in Higher Education, Journal of Marketing for Higher Education, 8(2), pp. 29-35.

Yost, M. & Tucker, S.L. (1995) Tangible Evidence in Marketing a Service: the value of a campus visit in choosing a college, Journal of Marketing for Higher Education, 6, pp. 47-67.

(See also P. Gibbs, forthcoming (2004, Kluwer Academic), *Trusting in the University*.)

Appendix 3

COSTING, FUNDING AND SUSTAINING OXFORD

1 This OxCHEPS/The Ulanov Partnership Project Report was first reported in The Economist *(15/1/04) under the headline: '***A bargain: The cost of an undergraduate***' (©The Economist Newspaper and the Economist Group)*

WHAT does it really cost to educate an undergraduate at Oxford University? Not £3,000 ($5,500) a year, the top fee the government will allow Oxford to charge if its education bill—and indeed, the prime minister—survives. A privately financed think-tank, the Oxford Centre for Higher Education Policy Studies (OXCHEPS), has commissioned the Ulanov Partnership, a consultancy, to take apart the university's finances. It has come up with an answer in an unpublished report: £18,600. That figure excludes accommodation and catering (not covered by the government's cap), and ranges from £17,100 for an arts degree to £20,900 for science. The number depends crucially on how core research costs are allocated: knock them out, and costs per undergraduate fall to £13,800. Either way, the current tuition fee of £1,125 pays less than 10% of the cost of educating a student.

The funding gap helps to explain why Oxford dons are paid one-third as much per teaching hour as their American counterparts. More important, they carry a much heavier teaching load than American dons. They have roughly twice as many undergraduates per don as Harvard or Princeton and less help with their teaching duties. At Harvard, there are half as many teaching assistants as dons; in Oxford, hardly any. Overall, Harvard appears to employ about five academic support staff (librarians, research technicians and so on) per don; Oxford employs just over two. Dons who flee Oxford for America often complain that what drove them was not the pay but the lack of help with mundane chores such as photocopying.

One implication is that Oxford is paying its way much more than is generally realised. OXCHEPS reckons that 58% of the costs of teaching come not from students or government but from private money such as conference earnings and endowment income. If the bill to raise fees fails, that will have to increase. Oxford is considering increasing the proportion of overseas students from 7% now to 12% in 2008, and the number of postgraduates (who pay more) from 5,400 now to 7,000.

The study has looked not just at Oxford's finances but also at its students' backgrounds. Oxford tends to be at the sharp end of Labour rhetoric because it is assumed to be full of grandees. But only 17% of Oxford students come from families with incomes of £60,000 a year or more; 42% from families with £40,000-50,000 a year.

2. *Subsequently, the Project Report was circulated (as set out below in paragraph 7) and commented upon in various newspapers, viz:* Times Higher *(12/2/04, 20/2/04, 11/3/04 & 29/3/04),* Guardian *(14/2/04),* Independent *(14/2/04 & 11/3/04),* Telegraph *(14/2/04, lead story on the front page), and in* The Independent on Sunday *(15/2/04). 16. It was also discussed in a* Financial Times *leader on 26/3/04: 'The fees debate is much ado about far too little...a heated debate over illusory principles...The current parliamentary fracas is both foolish and irrelevant...'*

3. *The* Times Higher *(20/2/04) also reported the Russell Group view on the proposed £3K cap:*

In an interview with *The Times Higher,* Michael Sterling – chairman of the Russell Group and vice-chancellor of Birmingham University – said the government's plans to boost university funding by charging tuition fees of up to £3,000 a year from 2006 would do nothing to help England's best universities compete internationally – a key government aim... "The gap left by the £3,000 cap on top-up fees is huge", he said. "It leaves us less than two-thirds of the way towards closing the funding gap with America. If the government gets its top-up fees legislation through Parliament, I'm looking forward to seeing its plans to close the gap."...Professor Sterling said that by 2008-09, when all three year groups of students at any university would be paying top-up fees, the unit of resource per student would rise by £1,700 per student to £7,200 – some £3,800 per student less than the US. Professor Sterling said he agreed with the thrust of an independent think-tank's report last week that analysed the funding gap faced by Oxford University...A spokeswoman for Oxford said the report was independent but the University was confident that the figures were accurate.

110

4. In The Independent on Sunday *(15/2/04, 'Comment') Sir David Davies, the key funder of this OxCHEPS Project, spelt out the financial crisis facing top universities:*

The debate on the funding of higher education has been transfixed by government efforts to appease its backbenchers, and by the failure of the Tory opposition to provide any worthwhile policy... I graduated from Oxford in the early 1960s. When the time came for me to return a small part of my debt...I became aware of an uneasy malaise that permeated parts of the University with murmuring of financial problems. Could it be that Oxford was on track to become a second-tier body...? The only way to get to the bottom of the matter was to commission an independent report. What seemed to be missing was informed consideration of the core of the problem...What is the cost of maintaining UK universities' position 'among the best in the world'? How can this cost be met? Unfortunately it has become clear that the Government's Higher Education Bill will not provide the answer... The outlook for top universities is grim...These institutions are way down the financial slippery slope...

*5. William Rees-Mogg (*Times, *16/2/04) picked up the theme:*

One can no more pretend that a great university is not an elitist institution than that Manchester United is an egalitarian employer of footballers. The problem is to bring together a critical mass of exceptional talent, and to maintain it. The danger now is that economic pressures are undermining those British universities that are internationally recognised as belonging to the highest category... They are great universities in the full sense. Their health is essential to the whole university community and, more broadly, to the vitality of British culture... The Oxford Centre for Higher Education Policy Studies...has now published a report on the funding of Oxford that shows the university is, indeed, under-funded... The Government's proposals, if they pass into law, will be worth _18 million. That is plainly not enough. It comes to only 3 per cent of the University's turnover... Oxcheps proposes a plan for uncapped tuition fees, matched by generous bursaries... This follows the US pattern of high fees for wealthy families, but entry regardless of ability to pay...Universities are independent institutions. The State has every reason to support them financially... But, when it comes to paying for tuition, the taxpayer has no reason to support those whose family incomes are three or four times the national average, or even higher. The universities should be set free to charge what they think is desirable...Universities should not charge fees to those families who cannot afford them; they should charge only the rich at their full rate. But they should be put in an independent position where they can compete on level terms in a world market for excellence.

6. Independently, the Rector of Imperial College (Sir Richard Sykes), in his typically forthright style, has made the same point about funding the top-tier UK HEIs: if the Government wants to prime the economy and also achieve value-for-money from its HE budget, it should concentrate taxpayer funding on sustaining the existing world-class universities and drop the unaffordable goal of 50% participation in HE which is 'draining the system', causing 'unbelievable stresses', and 'diverting resources to third-class institutions' (Financial Times, 11/3/04).

7. The OxCHEPS Report is summarised below.

8. The full OxCHEPS Report can be reviewed at, and down-loaded from, the OxCHEPS web-site (oxcheps.new.ox.ac.uk) at 'Papers' (Item 13).

COSTING, FUNDING AND SUSTAINING HIGHER EDUCATION A Case Study of Oxford University - Highlights

Independent research conducted by the Oxford Centre for Higher Education Policy Studies (OxCHEPS) and The Ulanov Partnership has some startling conclusions. OxCHEPS is a non-political think tank dedicated to higher education and independent of Oxford University. The Ulanov Partnership is an international strategy and management consultancy for the university and non-profit sectors.

- First-ever comprehensive financial model and analysis of Oxford University
- Research based on budgets and balance sheets of Oxford University and its Colleges
- Comparisons made with leading public and private universities in the United States

Key Findings

- Oxford spends two-thirds less educating each undergraduate than US counterparts
- Typical education of an undergraduate at Oxford works out to an average cost of £18,600 p.a.
- Of this amount, only 6 percent is currently paid through tuition fees by a Home/EU undergraduate
- Of the remaining 94 percent, Oxford contributes roughly half from private sources, with the Government contributing the other half
- The top tier of UK higher education is in crisis
- Per-student public funding has halved system-wide in the past 20 years
- Current funding system for Oxford will lead to a £19m education deficit in five years, growing to £35m in eight years
- Compared to other globally leading universities, Oxford faces an additional £99m - £231m annual 'Aspiration Gap' of
  - Significantly lower academic pay than at US competitors
  - More demanding teaching loads
  - Half as many dons per undergraduate than Harvard/Princeton
  - Much fewer academic support staff
  - Lower levels of infrastructure maintenance
- The UK Government's Higher Education Bill will NOT solve the funding crisis
- £3,000 in tuition fees is an arbitrary price cap
- Education costs increase faster than the Retail Price Index (RPI)
- With the Government plan, Oxford will have an education deficit of £14m by 2012, accelerating thereafter

Impact

- Oxford is losing its world-beating academic status
- Further cost cutting will compromise the quality of education
- Internal plans project increased numbers of (higher paying) overseas students – with the loss of 600-1,400 places for Home undergraduate students
- US universities with better resources and bursaries are already recruiting some of the brightest UK undergraduates
- Academic staff leave for the US in a vicious cycle of diminishing resources

Alternative – Uncapped Access Model

- Uncapped Access Model promotes greater access and generates significantly greater funds for Oxford
- Needs-blind admissions and needs-based financial aid based on a progressive model of uncapped fees
    - Extends fee-free education beyond Government's plans to students from families earning less than £30,000
    - Charges lower fees than Government proposal for those from families earning up to £45,000
    - Contributes £10m more in fees to Oxford than Government proposal

Index

Index of Subjects

Printed in the United Kingdom
by Lightning Source UK Ltd.
103224UKS00001B/307-333